THE BASIC FEATURES OF POSTCOMMUNIST CAPITALISM IN EASTERN EUROPE

THE BASIC FEATURES OF POSTCOMMUNIST CAPITALISM IN EASTERN EUROPE

Firms in Hungary, The Czech Republic, and Slovakia

Lawrence Peter King

Westport, Connecticut
London

Library of Congress Cataloging-in-Publication Data

King, Lawrence P.
    The basic features of postcommunist capitalism in Eastern
  Europe : firms in Hungary, the Czech Republic, and Slovakia /
  Lawrence Peter King.
      p. cm.
  Includes bibliographical references and index.
  ISBN 0–275–96839–1 (alk. paper)
    1. Capitalism—Europe, Eastern.   2. Post-communism—Europe,
  Eastern.   3. Europe, Eastern—Economic policy—1989–
  I. Title.
HC244 .K485   2001
330.12′2′0947—dc21   00–023310

British Library Cataloguing in Publication Data is available.

Library of Congress Catalog Card Number: 00–023310
ISBN: 0–275–96839–1

First published in 2001

Praeger Publishers, 88 Post Road West, Westport, CT 06881
An imprint of Greenwood Publishing Group, Inc.
www.praeger.com

Printed in the United States of America

The paper used in this book complies with the
Permanent Paper Standard issued by the National
Information Standards Organization (Z39.48-1984).

10 9 8 7 6 5 4 3 2 1

This book is dedicated to Barbara and Jerome Lichtman, William and Pat King, and Marta King.

Contents

List of Tables

List of Appendices

1

Introduction: Making Capitalism in Eastern Europe

The revolutions that toppled Communism in Eastern Europe effected such vast and radical disruptions in the world's ideological, political and economic structures that Fukuyama's announcement that history had ended seemed momentarily plausible (Fukuyama 1992). The great alternative to capitalist democracy had failed, seemingly leaving the secular world only one political and economic model to emulate.[1] However, as the "planned economies" disintegrated, the analytical dichotomy of "plan" and "market" lost its relevance, and the existing variations between different capitalist economies became more obvious. A new field of study, "comparative capitalism," became a necessity. This book intends to contribute to this domain by analyzing both the process of the transition to, and the resulting structure of, capitalism in Eastern Europe.

While there have been many completed, as well as attempted, transitions to capitalism throughout history, the transition to capitalism in Eastern Europe was unique. First, in Eastern Europe an attempt was made to create a capitalist system in a context with few indigenous capitalists. Unlike the many other attempts throughout history to create a capitalist system without capitalists,[2] no large-scale class of private owners of any type existed, such as agrarian elites or prosperous peasants, that could be more or less easily transformed into capitalists. Only a modest group of small-scale "socialist entrepreneurs" had been allowed to develop in Hungary, a class that was almost nonexistent in most other Communist societies such as Czechoslovakia. One problem encountered in the transition concerned the need to create a group of private owners—the pillar of any "capitalist" economy.

One might expect that this lack of a domestic ownership class would pose enormous problems during the process of privatizing the state-owned enterprises that dominated the economy. Margaret Thatcher herself managed to privatize only 20 firms in 10 years, a number representing just 5 percent of the United Kingdom's gross domestic product. If England encountered such difficulty, how could the postcommunist societies, having no comparable class of capitalists available to buy these properties and possessing no functioning capital market to facilitate this activity, accomplish such an enormous task?

The tremendous problems involved in accomplishing this mission were further complicated by the historically unprecedented fact that the transition to capitalism was occurring in societies which had experienced massive capital accumulation. There is universal agreement that this inherited capital stock suffered from "gigantism" or "diseconomies of scale" and was terribly outdated technologically. For these reasons, the existing set of enterprises could not be easily integrated into the world economy.[3]

Not only did this pattern of socialist accumulation create an outdated industrial structure, it also created a culture or a pattern of interactions not typically associated with a private market economy. The people of Eastern Europe were socialized within a system in which "the state" and "clientelistic ties" were all-important.[4] Any essential social activity required permission and/or resources from some part of the state/party hierarchy. Gaining access to this state/party hierarchy involved forging clientelistic links with some patron.

Therefore, those seeking to forge a market economy from the ruins of Communism faced an incredibly daunting task. They had to create a "private economy" without the presence of a preexisting group of "private owners," while restructuring the vast majority of enterprises to make them competitive on world markets. This task was to be accomplished by agents socialized in a noncapitalist system.

ANALYZING THE TRANSITION FROM SOCIALISM TO CAPITALISM: ECONOMIC AND SOCIOLOGICAL APPROACHES

Given the enormous difficulties facing those who wished to transform socialism into capitalism, one must inquire as to how this formidable task would be accomplished. Economics suggests one answer, and sociology another. Economics, as a discipline, tends to ignore both history and social structure, relying instead on the role of "markets" and the drive for "efficiency" to explain the development of economic organizations.[5]

This position is summed up succinctly by Jeffrey Sachs, perhaps the world's most influential economist, who views reforms in postcommunist society as "the generalized introduction of market forces which will guide most of the . . . restructuring" (Sachs 1991: 3; see also Kosolowski 1992; Lipton and Sachs 1990; Fischer and Gelb 1991; Blanchard et al. 1993: 10–11; Carlin, Van Reenen, and Wolfe 1994: 72). Thus, economic restructuring assumes a *tabula rasa* in which, once the correct incentives are found, everything else follows. Such reasoning implicitly accepts a model of atomized economic individuals. If one can simply change the "rules of the game," all actors will immediately and easily respond to the new set of incentives.

Sociologists, on the other hand, see economic life as consisting of individuals embedded in concrete networks (Granoveter 1985). From a sociological standpoint, it is highly improbable that a social system heavily dominated by the state and clientelistic relationships could be almost immediately transformed into a system with a minimalist state and an economy in which actors engage in "arm's length" market activity. Long-established networks existed and certain ways of doing things had become habituated (see Bordieu 1977). Even when institutions change rapidly, they most often still bear at least some mark of the previous system.

Sociologists did not influence the process of transition. Intellectual leadership for the transition was provided by economists. Therefore, the restructuring of the postcommunist[6] economies along capitalist lines was intended to be guided primarily by market forces, rather than the state or networks. And, to a certain extent, the postcommunist state in Eastern Europe has fulfilled its neoclassical mandate. In an attempt to live up to its Anglo-American model of capitalism, little in the way of an official or unofficial industrial policy has been created. The policies of the first postcommunist governments—stabilization, liberalization and privatization—were intended to allow "efficiency" considerations to shape the organizations of the new capitalist economies. By creating "private property" and introducing market competition, so the theory goes, economic actors would be forced to compete over scarce resources. Without the state to prop up inefficient actors, only the capable would survive. This formula, it was asserted, would quickly create "normal" economies as found in Europe and America.

Since the restructuring of the economy would have to be accomplished through the operation of market forces, a special role was assigned to foreign capital in an attempt to facilitate this process. Foreign investment would serve as the *deus ex machina* by performing all those tasks that the "developmental state" would. Thus, the drastically needed and fantastically expensive industrial restructuring that Eastern Europe would need to "catch up" with the West, or as Sachs puts it, to experience a "democratically based increase in living standards," was to be accomplished with the help of the "world market." This argument was summed up elegantly in a speech at the Collegium Budapest in 1995, when the U.S. Ambassador to Hungary stated,

I have often been asked why there isn't a new Marshall Plan to help Central and Eastern Europe. Well, there is—it is here—and it is called private foreign investment. . . . Foreign investment creates jobs, enhances productivity, generates economic growth, and raises the standard of living. It brings new technology, new management techniques, new markets, new products, and better ways of doing business. (quoted in Gowan 1995: 10)

Unfortunately, "actually existing foreign capital" has not been much more successful than "actually existing socialism" in solving Eastern Europe's problems. Foreign direct investment (FDI) simply was not substantial enough to get the job done. FDI inflow per capita in 1995 U.S. dollars was $346 in Hungary, $243 in the Czech Republic, and $47 in Slovakia. The average for Central and Eastern Europe, including the former Soviet Union, was only $31.50. Thus, FDI in the region has been generally quite low compared to other regions. In England, for example, the corresponding figure was $513.50 (United Nations 1996: 64).

Market forces, therefore, undoubtedly play a major role in explaining the shape of the economic transition. However, they need to be complemented by investigating a variety of forces that traditionally belong to the domain of sociology. Analyses of economic organizations in the capitalist West that focus exclusively on the market and efficiency have come under increasing attack (see Roy 1997; Perrow 1986). Similarly, this book argues that postcommunist capitalism has been created through many practices that are far removed from considerations of the "market" and "efficiency."

THE ROLE OF THE STATE AND POLITICAL POWER

Sociologists have long insisted that the state and political power play a major role in shaping economic organizations in the West (Fligstein 1990; Roy 1997; Powell and Dimagio 1983). One can expect, therefore, that these forces play an even greater role in postcommunist society given its statist past. Indeed, despite the neoliberal rhetoric, the postcommunist state has had a major and complex causal effect on the transformation of property in Eastern Europe. State ownership has had consequences that affect both the distribution of property rights and the structure of governance systems. This point has been stressed by David Stark, one of the leading analysts of the Eastern European economies (Stark 1989, 1992, and 1996; Stark and Bruszt 1995). For Stark, state ownership is manifested both in the continued ownership of state enterprises, and in the more interesting cases when state ownership combines with private ownership, creating what he terms "recombinant property." This, Stark insists, profoundly influences the operation of firms in the postcommunist economy.

While Stark emphasizes the role of state ownership, Staniszkis (1991) argues that political power shapes the emerging private economy. Staniszkis' account of the economic transformation of the postcommunist countries stands in exact opposition to the logic employed by neoclassical economists and the sociologists who mirror their arguments. One such sociologist is Victor Nee (1989, 1996) whose "market transition" thesis argues that the new ownership class emerges from the "bottom up," originating from efficiency-driven market processes outside the Communist power structure.[7] Staniszkis, in contrast, sees a "top down" process whereby political power held during the communist period became the primary asset used by the *nomenclatura* to turn itself into a grand bourgeoisie.

Writing about the Polish experience, Staniszkis observes the emergence of "political capitalism" in which the old *nomenclatura* becomes an ownership class which utilizes "various combinations of power and capital" (Staniszkis 1991: 38).

The basic idea posits that members of the *nomenclatura* are able to convert their political power into private ownership. This account, in fact, expresses the most dominant journalistic interpretation of the transition process. Similarly, when economists are pushed to the wall to acknowledge nonmarket factors that shaped the actual process of change, they usually opt for a variant of the political capitalism thesis. For example, Frydman, Murphy, and Rapaczynski (1996) describe the transformation of the *nomenclatura* into a "kleptoclatura."

In addition to simply becoming owners, Staniszkis argues that former *nomenclatura* have been able to set up special firms, insert themselves in the sphere of circulation of capital, and make a profit. "In this brokerage activity the 'basic capital' is access to information and means of transportation; being in the nomenclatura affords both" (1991: 41).

Thus, special attention to the use of political power and the role of the state in the transformation of property in Eastern Europe is warranted. This involves a double process that operates both from the top down as well as from the bottom up. The top-down aspect involves the use of "state power" to shape enterprises to reach some state-defined goal. The bottom-up process occurs with the private appropriation of "state power" by private individuals in a process that I, borrowing from Staniszkis (1991), and Weber (1978), will call "political capitalism."

The top-down process occurs when the state uses various means to affect the survival of firms in the pursuit of "state interests" such as keeping unemployment down. I call this process "subterranean redistribution." The term "redistribution" is borrowed from Konrad and Szelenyi (1979), who in turn borrowed it from Polanyi (1957). It refers to the centralization and subsequent redistribution of essential economic resources. For example, in ancient Egypt the pharaoh's bureaucracy moved the means of subsistence around the empire,[8] just as under "actually existing socialism" the party/state hierarchy centralized investment resources and then redistributed them according to the dictates of the five-year plan. These societies are examples of "redistributive" economies, because the most important economic goods are allocated by the political center, not by markets (although there were certainly smaller, localized markets).[9] Thus, this type of activity involves "redistribution." It is also "subterranean" because the post-communist governments do not advertise this type of activity, and they use unofficial or "hidden" methods to redistribute resources, such as placing informal pressure on banks to extend credit to certain companies. These governments wish to keep this type of state activity underground and hidden, in order to present an attractive ideological profile to the EU, NATO, IMF, World Bank, and various lending groups.

The "bottom-up" process occurs when private individuals "privatize" state power. That is, individuals use clientelistic ties to people with political power or bureaucratic authority to influence firm restructuring or firm survival. Thus, in addition to the issues surrounding continued state ownership, the role of the private appropriation of political power must be considered an important factor in shaping the emergence of the market economy.

Clearly, the restructuring of firms depends heavily on the formation of clientelistic networks between enterprise managers and state managers. This network effect provides only one example of the importance of networks in the restructuring of property.

NETWORKS

Just as the role of the state in shaping firms has been extensively studied in the West, a massive literature analyzing the effects of networks in shaping organizations also exists.[10] Indeed, David Stark also stresses the role of networks in his analysis. David Stark's notion of recombinant property is meant to suggest the creation of dense networks between the personnel of different, nominally separate enterprises. This type of property is created by breaking up enterprises into many corporations. They are "nominally independent," having their own boards of directors and balance sheets. Controlling shares in these corporations are "typically held by the public enterprises themselves" (Stark 1996: 1005): top- and mid-level managers/professionals, other limited-liability companies that often orbit around the same enterprise, limited-liability companies that orbit around some other enterprise, or another main enterprise. Thus, there are "horizontal ties of cross-ownership intertwined with vertical ties of nested holdings"(1007).

The new property form in Hungary consists not only of the recombinant firm, but the network ties linking all these firms as well (1009). In an earlier paper, Stark labeled "this emergent form a *recombinet*, an appropriate hybrid term designating the hybrid phenomenon of a *network of recombinant property*" (1993: 14). Stark argues that the terms "vertical" and "horizontal" integration taken from the industrial organization literature, fail to express the complex manner in which property is actually being recombined. Terms that describe networks (such as extensivity, density, tight or loose coupling, strong or weak ties, structural holes, and so on) should be used instead. Stark concludes that "The existence of pervasive inter-enterprise ownership and the emergence of the recombinet organizational form suggests, moreover, that the proper analytic unit, because it is the actual economic unit of the Hungarian economy, is not the individual firm but a network of firms" (1993: 14). In a sense, informal networks based on reciprocity between firm managers and/or cross-ownership blur firm boundaries and partially replace market relationships.

Stark's work is the essential starting point of my analysis. It emphasizes the importance of networks in shaping the postcommunist transition, and it pays direct attention to the incredibly important phenomenon of cross-ownership. More generally, it focuses attention on the study of "real," as opposed to exclusively "formal," categories of property, and the possibility of finding many distinct forms of property beyond a simple "private/public" distinction.

BOUNDED RATIONALITY

The final insight from the sociological tradition that must be brought to bear on the transformation of property in postcommunist society concerns information and knowledge. Sociologists have long insisted that the assumption of "perfect information" in neoclassical theory is one that should never be made. March and Simon's classic statement on "bounded rationality" (1958) specifies various limits to the informational/decision-making processes of firms. One of their claims is that the most significant economic information is obtained at the firm's boundaries, and is known mostly by firm insiders.

The restructuring of the firms, then, occurs in a situation where firm insiders have a monopoly of specific knowledge about their firms, their firms' assets, and their firms' environment. My research shows that the restructuring of firms in postcommunist society occurred under conditions that allowed former socialist-era managers to take advantage of their local knowledge of their firms, as well as their ability to run these firms without effective supervision, in order to create new firms in relative secrecy. For example, a very pervasive pattern exists in which the management of a division of a state-owned enterprise sets up an independent firm and then funnels resources from the state-owned firm to the privately held firm through a variety of mechanisms. Much of the restructuring of property occurred in these quite unusual ways as a result of such informational asymmetries.

This book argues that the transformation of property, and therefore the transition from socialism to capitalism in Eastern Europe, is an active process whereby economic managers, under conditions of extreme inequalities of information, use networks for a variety of purposes. These networks include: (1) linking firms to engage in productive activity and share risk; (2) obtaining the allocations of valued goods (especially investment capital); (3) manipulating institutional ownership to protect the control exercised by firm insiders; (4) teaming up with outside owners (usually foreign, but sometimes domestic); and (5) capturing state power for the advantage of the firm or firm insiders.

The proper understanding of the process of the transition in postcommunist Eastern Europe is important on levels beyond mere intellectual interest. If the process has been driven largely by "efficiency" considerations and can be explained adequately with neoclassical economics, this would indicate that an optimal use of societal resources has been achieved. Therefore, any interference in the supposedly "self-regulating markets" would create a less efficient outcome. In this scenario, the state should be a minimalist one and its only task should be to provide a stable economic environment.

However, to the extent that the transition to capitalism in Eastern Europe is driven by processes far removed from markets and efficiency—such as clientelistic relations or political power—then the state might legitimately be expected to intervene more actively in the process of economic restructuring. At stake in this analysis, then, is the legitimacy of the use of neoclassical theory to inspire policy decisions that guide transitions from socialism to capitalism.

STUDYING THE TRANSITION

This book will explore the postcommunist economies by studying the primary unit of economic life, the postcommunist enterprise. The now-dominant methodological position among social scientists insists that one establish the micro-foundations that under-lie macro-sociological phenomena. To understand the market economy, therefore, one might reasonably start by understanding its constituent elements—the most important being firms or enterprises as Coase (1937) observed long ago.[11] This focus on the firm contrasts with a tendency to focus on the *individual* level of analysis, which is typical of both neoclassical economics and mainstream stratification research in sociology. An individual is, occasionally, the primary unit of economic action (for example, a self-employed worker in the service industry). More often, however, the primary produc-tive unit is a family enterprise or some other type of firm. Under conditions of classical capitalism, where ownership and control typically lay with individual entrepreneurs, and labor is provided by "formally free" labor, a proposal to study the individual to elu-cidate the workings of the economy might be expected. In the situation of a transition from a socialist economy to a capitalist economy, however, this is methodologically unsound because it presupposes the forms of property and integrative mechanisms that presumably characterized the capitalism of the West a century ago.

This focus on the enterprise also supplies insights unattainable from the exclu-sive use of macroeconomic indicators to analyze the transition. A great deal of skepticism is warranted when using state-generated statistics, especially in cross-country comparisons within the postcommunist world (see Dobosiewicz 1992: xii). While macroeconomic indicators can tell us that countries in Eastern Europe have experienced a severe and protracted recession, or have recently resumed a positive growth rate, it is unclear to what extent *creative* destruction, as opposed to permanent destruction or deindustrialization, has occurred. An analysis of the firm could reveal that, even though the economy as a whole has suffered, some emerging postcommunist firms are capable of self-sustaining economic growth. In general, macro-level indicators can tell us nothing about the emerging forms of property or the industrial organization of various markets. Furthermore, they can tell us almost nothing about the structure of the economy, or even about the real differences between the organization of the economy in the various countries.

A close look at Table 1.1 demonstrates how little information macroeconomic statistics give us about the economic transition in Eastern Europe. Working from the neo-orthodox[12] position that capitalist economic structures lead to economic development, the data in Table 1.1 would imply that Slovakia has had the great-est transformation in the direction of Western capitalism. However, as anyone familiar with the region would argue, Slovakia has undoubtedly had the least

Table 1.1
Some Macroeconomic Indicators in Hungary, The Czech Republic, and Slovakia

	Hungary	*Czech Rep.*	*Slovakia*
GNP change 1989–96	– 8.12%	– 9.66%	– 8.06%
Inflation 1989–96	382.81%	273.08%	287.68%
Avg. Budget/ GDP 1989–96	6.13%	0.43%	1.08%
Ext. Debt/person 1995	$3,107.84	$1,601.94	$1,094.34
FDI/person 1996	$973.92	$486.21	$215.10

Source: Compiled from the Economist Intelligence Unit; OECD Economic Outlook 1995; UNCTAD 1995.

movement in this direction among the three countries in question. Furthermore, a clearly negative association between FDI and positive macroeconomic indicators also exists, a finding that contradicts the neoclassical position. This type of macroeconomic data is simply too aggregate to be of much use when trying to determine the shape of the new economies.

If the study of the transition from socialism to capitalism should proceed neither at the individual level nor at the macro-level of analysis, the question arises why the individual firm should be the object of study and not, as David Stark suggests, the network of firms. While Stark's account suggests that at least some actual production seems to take place through a network of firms, this does not lead inevitably to the conclusion that one should study the network of firms *as opposed* to the individual firms. Indeed, the study of the individual firm is necessary for a meaningful understanding of the network of firms. One can only study networks of firms by starting the analysis with individual firms, determining whether or not they are actually embedded in networks, and if so, the particular nature of those networks. My research shows that while some firms are embedded in inter-firm networks, others are not. To argue by analogy, a biologist studying the nervous system would not study only the synoptic connections between individual cells, but would study the different types of nerve cells as well. An understanding of the network presupposes an understanding of its constituent elements.

THE LOGIC OF THE COUNTRY COMPARISON

Why study the transition in Eastern Europe? And why study Hungary and the former Czechoslovakia? First, the countries of Eastern Europe, among the postcommunist countries, have the best chance of accomplishing a successful transition to capitalism and "joining" the European capitalist system. They are both literally and figuratively closest to Western Europe. These countries possessed the highest degree of capitalist development prior to the institutionalization of the Communist system, and they have the greatest opportunity to achieve international economic cooperation now. Thus, I expect that the Central European economies, among all the countries of the postcommunist world, will have produced the most change in the direction of capitalism for a variety of reasons: their proximity to Western Europe, their functioning democracy, and their relative attractiveness to foreign capital.[13]

Due to this configuration of reasons, this book uses Hungary and the former Czechoslovakia as a sample frame to study the different species of postcommunist firms. Beyond this, however, a comparison of the experience of Hungary to the experience of the former Czechoslovakia provides an additional valuable exercise in understanding the development of capitalist systems. The former Czechoslovakia, having never experienced a significant period of economic reform, offers a useful point of comparison with Hungary. Hungary, in contrast, experienced numerous market-oriented reforms starting with the New Economic Mechanism in 1968, and extending up until the transition.

Most observers hypothesized that prior experience with markets would create economic units more compatible with advanced capitalism. The comparison between Hungary and the former Czechoslovakia will allow this claim to be assessed. In addition, the former Czechoslovakia enjoys much greater economic sovereignty than Hungary vis-à-vis international economic organizations since, unlike Hungary, it never accumulated a huge external debt during the reform period. We might expect this to give the Czech and Slovak states more maneuverability than their Hungarian counterpart when dealing with foreign capital and international economic institutions (like the IMF and the World Bank). This, in turn, might alter the relationship that exists between the government and enterprises. Certainly, the lack of a large external debt significantly increases the potential for domestic "ownership solutions," since a large foreign debt predisposed the Hungarian government to sell state assets for cash to service their debt. This often meant selling state-owned enterprises to foreign capital.

While a causal analysis of the different outcomes in the three countries under consideration is one goal of this book, it is not the primary goal. Because an appraisal of the state of the postcommunist firm has never been seriously attempted, the most important task of this book is to establish both the various characteristics of the major types of postcommunist firms, and the various processes by which they emerge. In essence, I am seeking to create a taxonomy of the postcommunist firm.

SOURCES OF DATA

The emerging Eastern European capitalist systems have barely been studied. Moreover, they have been changing rapidly. Therefore, methodologically, I saw my task as similar to that of an evolutionary biologist who stumbles upon a quickly evolving ecosystem, such as a previously isolated tropical island that is undergoing development for the first time. The task of such a biologist would be to survey as widely as possible the various flora and fauna, so as to establish a baseline to which to compare future developments. This is not the type of activity that is normally undertaken by sociologists, since the discipline tends to emphasize the testing of theories through quantitative techniques over the discovery of new phenomena. However, one must first understand the dimensions of a new phenomenon before one can explain why it came about—let alone make statistical inferences about its causes. Because I felt so much needed to be understood about the postcommunist economy, I wanted to get as big a picture as possible of the economic transformation in Eastern Europe. To this end, my strategy was to utilize all available data at different levels of depth—so that the analysis missed neither the forest nor the trees.

At the most shallow level I used state-generated statistics. Then, I used a variety of survey instruments, some of which I helped construct myself. (Appendix 1 describes these data sets.) Finally, I conducted interviews with firm-level actors (as described in Appendix 2). Whenever possible I confirmed the information I obtained through interviews with publicly available legal or financial records.

The interviews constituted the most important source of data. Although firm-level survey data is invaluable in establishing the broad contours of the types of firms in Eastern Europe, this type of data cannot truly capture the transformation of firms during postcommunism. Firm transformation must be understood as a process, as a particular sequence of events. To capture this phenomenon, histories of firms needed to be developed.

These histories of firms can only be obtained through case studies. In case-study research, as with other methods, one must balance breadth versus depth. Depth of research, accomplished most successfully through ethnographic techniques, increases one's ability to understand the detailed workings of social processes at the site of study.[14] However, it is reasonable to want breadth, or more "cases," because of the widely accepted recognition that most social processes have stochastic outcomes and that the findings in any given case may simply be atypical. By increasing the number of cases, one raises the generalizability of one's findings. Breadth also allows one to pose theoretical questions by providing ample opportunities for the comparison of cases.

In terms of the breadth-versus-depth trade-off in case studies, this book errs on the side of breadth. Because prior research created the expectation that there would be a great diversity of organizational forms and processes of transformation, I felt it would be better to cast my net widely and try to obtain reliable information on as many different types of firms as possible. Thus, I conceptualized this research as a first attempt to come to terms with the emergence of new capitalist systems in Eastern Europe, and in no sense do I view this as a definitive study of these systems. In a sense, this book establishes a research agenda for future work by creating a typology of the postcommunist firm, and uses this information to try to construct a model of Eastern European capitalism.

Ultimately, as the method of "thick description" recognizes, the "proof is in the pudding" (see Geertz 1985). It is up to the readers to judge whether the cases ring true, as well as whether my interpretation offers any insight into the questions I am seeking to answer. Personally, I was surprised at what the interviewees told me, especially about illegal activities, such as various methods of funneling resources out of firms. This increases my confidence in the validity of my data.

By using this method to establish a typology of different postcommunist firms, which will be presented and elaborated in the following chapter, my research has allowed me to construct a theory of the transformation of the postcommunist economy that moves beyond the insights provided by the prevailing social-scientific interpretations. Nee, Staniszkis, and Stark each capture part, but not all, of the emergent structures. Processes that look like market transition, political capitalism, and recombinant property are all present. Yet none of these explanations is sufficient. I attempt to offer an analysis which subsumes these findings, showing them to be part of a process of firm transformation that results in a unique system of capitalism in Eastern European.

These data will reveal that the transition in Eastern Europe indeed represents a shift to a capitalist system. With statistical survey data, and, more importantly, with more detailed case-study data, I show that state-owned property has been significantly transformed into "private" capital, meaning corporate property that is not under the direct ownership of the state. While some "private property" had always existed in Eastern Europe, it was restricted to very small-scale petty-bourgeois production. Now, the most important companies in the economy are not, for the most part, owned by the state or, even more significantly, under state control.

Even more important than the formal change in ownership, most economic units have become market-dependent, and live or die by their ability to maximize the price-cost ratio and sell their output on the market. They behave like market-dependent firms. Nonetheless, just as in the advanced capitalist economies of the West and East, the firms are imbedded in a variety of nonmarket structures which must be explicated.

THE ORGANIZATION OF THE BOOK

This book will be divided into five additional chapters. The second and third chapters will summarize my findings. I identify "strategies of transition" employed by postcommunist economic elites to transform property and acquire various property rights. These strategies, when aggregated, are primarily responsible for the structuring of the postcommunist capitalist systems. I also discuss the conditions under which different strategies are likely to be selected, and the resources used by actors to implement these strategies. I then present statistical evidence on the different types of property forms, as well as evidence for the existence of subterranean redistribution and the clientelistic access to financial resources.

The remaining chapters will take a closer look at some of the most important property forms that have developed. The fourth chapter delves into the ideologically loaded area of foreign direct investment, seeking to go beyond the typically Manichean conceptions of this phenomenon by specifying the numerous ways in which foreign capital plays a role in transforming property in Eastern Europe. The fifth chapter contemplates the role of management and employee buy-outs in the transition to private property. I show that this property form, which Jeffrey Sachs called an illegitimate "third way," has been quite pervasive.

Managers have been quite successful in gaining property rights. But to understand this process, one must look beyond the formal buy-out activity emphasized in the economic literature, and explore the many ways in which the transfer of various property rights occurs. In the conclusion, I explore the varied distribution of firm types in the different countries, and examine the relationship of different types of property to economic performance and long-term development.

NOTES

1. The only alternative seems to be religious fundamentalism, but this system has only seriously impacted some parts of the Islamic world.

2. Essentially all non-socialist attempts at modernization can be so construed.

3. This inadequate industrial organization resulted from the logic of accumulation in the Communist era. Politics, not economic efficiency or profitability, drove investment decisions. Thus, an industrial structure developed that maximized the power of those in the Communist party/state hierarchy (see Konrad and Szelenyi 1979). This was the root cause of the inefficient use of resources under Communist regimes. (For the classic explication of this dynamic, see Kornai 1980.)

4. According to Konrad and Szelenyi (1979), "statism" and "clientelism" pervaded Eastern Europe long before the emergence of Communism.

5. See Chandler 1970: 19; North 1990; Williamson 1975, 1981, 1985; Demsetz 1967; Demsetz and Lehn 1985; Alchian and Demsetz 1972; Fama and Jensen 1983: 227. The exception to this literature consists of the economic concept of path-dependency, in which prior decisions significantly constrain the shape of future decisions.

6. The decision to use the term "postcommunist" requires some explanation. This term has become quite loaded ideologically, and has shifted in meaning from referring to the entire society that was once ruled by Communist regimes to referring more generally to ex-members of the former Communist Party. I think that this meaning is unfortunate, for it denies the legacy of the Communist period in analyzing current Eastern European society. Even anti-Communist former political dissidents are "postcommunist," because their habits and practices were formed under Communist rule. Thus, this more restricted meaning of "postcommunism" implicitly denies the importance of history in studying the transition process.

7. Nee formulated his theory to explain the development of capitalism in China, but his argument has been widely extended to Eastern Europe (see Szelenyi and Kostello 1996; Rona-Tas 1994).

8. The Egyptian bureaucracy centralized grain extracted from the peasantry and shipped it around the empire.

9. In the West, "redistribution" cannot be considered a primary "integrative mechanism," despite the existence of the welfare state. The West's welfare institutions merely intervene to redistribute incomes after market activity has taken place. The state does not direct a very significant flow of capital as it did under socialism. (Of course, state expenditures are huge, but they don't for the most part involve the actual production or sale of commodities.)

10. There is a network literature on interlocks, flexible production, labor markets, and ethnic enclaves. See Powell and Smith-Doer (1994) for a review of this literature.

11. Also see Brenner (1986) on the micro-foundations of economic growth.

12. Chapter 6 provides a full discussion of what I call the "neo-orthodoxy" of economic development.

13. Indeed, Hungary accounted for 9,934 million and the Czech Republic for 5,008 million of the 33,565 million dollars worth of FDI in the region up through 1995 (United Nations 1996: 64).

14. See Burawoy (1986) and Burawoy and Krotov (1992) for outstanding examples of this methodology applied to Hungary and Russia.

2

Strategies of Transition to Capitalism in Eastern Europe

In the introductory chapter, I reviewed the various economic and sociological approaches to the transition from socialism to capitalism, and laid out my strategy for attempting to analyze the process of the transformation and the resulting structure of the postcommunist economy in Hungary, the Czech Republic and Slovakia. In this chapter I will summarize my findings on the process by which property has been created or transformed in the postcommunist period.

STRATEGIES OF TRANSITION

Based on my in-depth interviews in 69 firms in Hungary, the Czech Republic, Slovakia and Slovenia during 1995, 1996, and 1998, I identify different strategies by which firm insiders, primarily former Communist-era managers, cope with the transition and simultaneously create the new "private economy." These strategies consist of the former manager or group of managers utilizing networks they formed during the socialist period, by combining them with various "assets" from their own firms as well as their firm's environment. These strategies are by no means mutually exclusive, and are often combined in any given case. The end result of these strategies is (1) the personal accumulation of wealth by the insider or insiders; or (2) the transformation of part or all of the old state firm into a new "private" enterprise; or (3) the creation of completely new private firms. The different strategies create different types of firms, which will have different consequences for the functioning and developmental potential of postcommunist capitalism.

Upon learning the details of these findings, some inevitably demand a moral accounting. However, during the rightful euphoria over the collapse of the oppressive Communist regimes, some forgot that capitalism is not now, nor ever was, a particularly "fair" or just system. For capitalism to exist there must be capitalists as well as workers, those unfortunate many who are motivated to work by what Weber called the "dull whip of hunger." As Weber observed, one of the essential steps in the historical formation of what he called "modern economic capitalism" was the enclosures movement—the separation of the direct producers from their means of production and means of subsistence (1946). What was common land used by all in the community was captured by the few, turning it into private property.

This process of creating private property out of common property has occurred in the creation of postcommunist capitalism no less than in the initial rise of capitalism in Western Europe. The following strategies detail the mechanisms by which this was accomplished. In so doing, the temptation to make moral judgments on these strategies is inevitable. However, I find Weber's injunction to value neutral research important: values should influence what you choose to study, but once this is decided, they should be bracketed as much as possible so as not to distort the research (Weber 1946). Many analyses of the transition are clearly normative, and in simply condemning ex-Communists as crooks they add very little of interest to the corpus of knowledge on transition. Their argument, to simplify drastically, is that the transition to Western-style democracy would be smooth and easy, if not for the corrupt and immoral ex-Communists and criminals engaged in corrupt and immoral activity. I try to avoid repeating this story.

Furthermore, in the context of the transition from Communism to capitalism, it is quite unclear from which moral vantage point one could make value judgments. Some of the managers of state-owned enterprises worked their whole lives in their companies. Faced with massive uncertainty during the transition period, who can blame them for wanting to preserve part of what they labored over, even if the means they selected were illegal or at least questionable? The most popular show in the Czech Republic, aired on the new private TV station NOVA, is *Dallas*, a show that stars the modern-day robber baron J. R. Ewing. This version of "capitalism" only reinforces what was learned under Communism—that capitalism is the unbridled pursuit of self-interest.

Finally, the type of research presented in this paper, based in part on "qualitative" techniques, demands an attitude of "naturalism" in order to be effective (Matza 1979). Part of this approach is to downplay the identification of "pathology" and focus more on "diversity" by adopting an appreciative stance.

IDEAL-TYPICAL STRATEGIES

The various strategies employed by managers (and sometimes employees) to survive the transition and transform firms all involve the combining of various resources. Table 2.1 lists these resources by the strategy employed.

Table 2.1
Ideal-typical Strategies and Resources

Strategy	Network	Resource political power	Financial power	Monopoly of information
Political capitalism	X	X		
Clientelistic finance	X		X	
Auto-cross-ownership	X		X	X
Partial self-ownership	X		X	
Simple satellite				X
By-pass satellite	X			X
Long-term satellite	X			X
Clone	X			X
MBO	X		X	X
EBO	X	X		X
MEBO	X	X		X
Foreign privatization	X		X	X
Joint-venture	X		X	X

STRATEGIES INVOLVING FOREIGN INVESTMENT

One set of strategies involves joining forces with foreign capital. Foreign investment was almost universally trumpeted as a necessary component to the remaking of the postcommunist economy. It was supposed to provide a vast array of benefits to the transforming economies, including the following: new technology; new quality-control techniques; new production techniques; a source of new jobs; access to Western markets; ties to global research and development networks; investment capital; small and medium-sized enterprises that were "missing" under socialism; competition to reduce the monopolization of the economy; new management techniques; new business standards and business ethics; Western standards of labor intensity; and entrepreneurial attitudes. (See the extended literature review in chapter 4.)

There are a number of ways in which foreign investment and local economic elites join forces. The most conspicuous type of foreign capital penetration consists of local managers assisting a multinational in the privatization of their company. Managers employing this strategy seek to become members of the upper management of a foreign multinational corporation (MNC) that privatizes an old state-owned enterprise. This is sometimes referred to as becoming a member of the "comprador intelligentsia," a term which implies that one grows wealthy by assisting foreigners in gaining economic control and dominance of one's own society (see Szelenyi 1995).

This is an attractive strategy for most managers, as the wealth and prestige that go along with being a member of the management of a foreign multinational are quite substantial. Managers are very rarely fired in this situation, and often earn extremely high salaries. In exchange for this treatment, socialist managers either provide exclusive and accurate information on the firm's capacities, or they hide firm assets so as to lower the price of privatization. While these services might not be highly ethical, the firm can be significantly strengthened by the capital, management expertise, and market access such privatization brings. The key to selecting this strategy involves having a buyer, a situation which exists only if the firm has some potential. Such potential might stem from a production process that can create commodities for an international market. Another source of potential, unfortunately, lies in a firm's market share and distribution system. Multinational firms suffering from excess capacity may choose to buy a firm simply to gain control over its market.

An example of this type of privatization comes from the Czechpharm joint-stock company. A large pharmaceutical company I studied in the Czech Republic was bought by an American pharmaceutical giant. The chief inducement, according to the CEO, resided in the firm's ability to make cyclosporine, a compound used in organ transplants. This company is one of only two plants in the world with this capacity, which was dubbed "the goose that lays the golden eggs" by one of my interviewees. In this case, the "*comprador intelligentsia*" (as they have been labeled by Szelenyi [1995]) had a much more positive effect than their Chinese counterparts who, in the mid-nineteenth century, helped saturate the Chinese market with British-supplied opium. The moment this large Czech firm was bought by the world's largest maker of generic drugs, its entire product line became available to the Czech Republic. Heretofore, the Czech Republic had suffered from a severely constricted diversity of drugs, due to the approach taken by the ministry of health, which "planned" the drug industry in the Czech Republic. On the other hand, many of these newly available drugs are very expensive by Eastern European standards.

While much discussion of the role of foreign direct investment in the transition economies envisions the large-scale privatization of state-owned enterprises, as in the case discussed above, the reality is much different. In Hungary, at least, foreign firms are smaller than average. They are overrepresented among firms with less than 100 employees, while they are quite underrepresented in the larger firms. My fieldwork indicated that much foreign investment took the form of small-scale joint ventures with former managers of state-owned enterprises.

This strategy is a variant of a very common method of establishing a private business, which I call establishing a "clone" company. A manager employing this strategy forms a private company that is a duplicate or "clone" of his or her old division (or part of a division) of the state-owned enterprise in which he or she formerly worked. The employees of the old enterprise provide the initial labor for the new enterprise.

The primary assets used in this strategy are the manager's specific knowledge of his or her firm, and his or her personal savings. The old manager takes part all of the network of human capital of a division (or a part of a division) of a state-owned enterprise, and establishes a legally separate company, with some or all of the same personnel, in the same business line as the old division. In this case what is "privatized" is the network of accumulated human capital, which is made more valuable by existing as a network of interdependent behavior. This includes contacts with old business partners, both foreign and domestic.

The foreign variety of this process consists of a manager (or group of managers) forming a clone company, and then negotiating a business arrangement between the clone company and a representative of a foreign company. Typically the manager met this representative during the socialist period. The foreign partner may become a part owner of the firm, thereby establishing a joint venture; or they may develop a symbiotic relationship based on the local firm selling the foreign firm's products. This process of joining foreign capital with local managers/nascent capitalists occurs on a much smaller scale than most other types of foreign direct investment, usually in companies employing 50 people or less.

A typical example of this property form is a medium-sized Hungarian manufacturer called Traffic JSC, which makes traffic lights and automated parking machines. The firm was founded in 1987 by the five top managers of a division of a state-owned enterprise that produced and developed a wide array of automated machines. The new company took none of the fixed assets from the parent company, choosing, rather, to take its human capital in the form of employees. The parent company, and as the interviewee described it the socialist elite, were opposed to this move. The new company, 100 percent privately owned by these founders, was started with a mere 200,000 HUF ($1,528 USD).

In this case, unlike the situation resulting from employing satellite strategies, a tight relationship exists between ownership and control. The five managers are also the sole owners and constitute the Board of Directors. The employees have no organization representing their interests and have no members on a Supervisory Board. In 1995, the five managers sold approximately one-quarter to one-third of their shares to an Austrian firm with whom they had had contact over an extensive period of time.

When studying this type of spin off company (which I refer to as "clone" company, but which can perhaps more accurately be called a "splinter" company), one can ask if this an example of a satellite revolving around a mother firm, as described by David Stark's theory of recombinant property (1996). The answer would be yes if this firm actively cooperated with the old mother company. However, just the opposite scenario existed. The CEO said that his firm's business strategy was to find the weak points of the old state company and exploit them. He commented that, at first, most purchasers did not want to do business with them because they were used to the old state-owned company. In spite of this, they managed to gain a 15 percent market share for their most important product, and 25 percent of the market for their second most important product. Some time after the founding of the firm, the mother company was bought by a German multinational which, along with another German multinational, now serves as their major competitor.

While there seems to be no network-production, the president of this company did admit making some small informal verbal agreements to cooperate with his competitors. He noted that, after the transition, severe competition caused all the firms to constantly undercut each other's prices. This became so severe that the companies were heading toward bankruptcy and vitiating the quality of their goods. Thus, the interviewee reported, in order to survive, this informal cooperation took place and the situation has now stabilized a bit. Indeed, this constitutes a move toward blurring firm boundaries and the creation of "recombinant property" as described by David Stark.[1]

Unlike those at Traffic JSC, many managers found it simply was not possible to utilize foreign capital as they strategized to reconfigure state-owned property. Thus, the other strategies they employed relied on creating domestic ownership. The most common approach was the "clone" company, as discussed above. This strategy can be selected whenever the economies of scale are small enough that a manager or group of managers can afford to "go independent." Often, these managers have specific technical skills that do not require expensive machinery to utilize.

SATELLITE COMPANIES

Equally interesting to the establishment of clone companies is the appropriation of "property," broadly conceived, from state-owned enterprises via satellite firms created and owned by managers.[2] Managers of state-owned firms, relying primarily on secrecy, are able to create side businesses in the form of satellites that revolve around the state-owned enterprise. Three different types of satellites exist. Short-term satellites perform imaginary work, such as "presentations" or "consulting," and serve as mechanisms for "privatizing" the financial assets of the firm. The key to the successful use of this strategy consists in controlling both ends of the transaction. Managers make contracts between their satellites and their own divisions and pay themselves for their nonexistent services. This is the only strategy that does not necessarily involve the use of a network—a manager can do it all on his or her own. However, other managers typically know what is going on and must be willing to be silent.

The second type of parasitic satellite tends to be more durable than the first, and operates on a much larger scale. Managers of state-owned firms form "satellite corporations" around the old state-owned or privatized firms. These satellite firms also utilize secrecy and are created during a period when there is no effective controlling owner. However, unlike the short-term parasitic satellites, they may continue to exist after ownership has been assigned. These firms are either subsidiaries of the "mother" company or are privately owned; whichever situation exists, the profit is taken by the managers (or manager-owners). Managers who employ this strategy profit by utilizing networks formed in the socialist period, and probably use kickbacks to establish themselves as either an intermediary company with the right to sell to the old company after taking a large portion of the profit margin, or as a competing company that takes the old company's markets.

An example of this strategy was pursued by the management of FoodCo., a Czech company. FoodCo. was founded in 1949 as a state-owned enterprise with a monopoly on the import and export of various foodstuffs. It was transformed into a shareholding company in 1969 and was thus owned by companies producing grain, other agricultural products and meat. FoodCo. lost its legally protected monopoly in 1989. FoodCo.'s old producers no longer had to sell through FoodCo., and foreign firms could sell directly to the food retail and wholesale companies.

FoodCo.'s response to this crisis, like three other old monopoly trading houses in the case studies, was to diversify their business activities. At the time of the transition, FoodCo. had a great accumulation of cash. My interviewee (the Chairman of the Board and Managing Director) reported that FoodCo. had a positive balance of more than two billion crowns with the state foreign trading bank and had been the bank's second biggest partner throughout the Communist period.

FoodCo.'s first wave of diversification, from 1990 to 1991, established daughter companies. After 1993 FoodCo. attempted a second round of diversification, this time under the direction of a foreign consultant who was also the Chairman of the Board of Directors. He brought in more foreign consultants to lead the diversification drive. During this process, and continuing until early 1995, members of the old management of FoodCo. started to establish daughter companies and other independent companies.

Through their old contacts with the foreign trading bank, these managers secured loans through FoodCo. for these businesses. These enterprises included banana, citrus and meat importing companies, a farm transport company, a sugar distribution company, a foreign debt service company, and a general trading company in the then war-torn Yugoslavia. By the end of 1994 FoodCo. owed the bank approximately 2.5 billion crowns ($78 million).

It was impossible to account for these loans, as the balance sheets of FoodCo. were literally destroyed by the old management. The interviewee was certain that this was not mere negligence, but rather the result of a deliberate move to cover up the massive graft that occurred in the company. The diversification plans involved huge investments (such as the establishment of a fast food restaurant opposite McDonald's in the heart of Prague) but resulted in almost no profits.

The healthy daughter companies, such as the meat, banana, and citrus importing companies, were able to carry out their business without any aid from FoodCo. Thus, FoodCo.'s management proposed that the company be liquidated. This move, my interviewee pointed out, would have totally destroyed any remaining evidence of the uncontrolled flow of funds out of the company.

The state foreign trading bank, as FoodCo.'s biggest creditor, had the right by law to block this liquidation. Instead of accepting such a massive loss, the bank entered the stock market, bought 76 percent of FoodCo.'s shares, and appointed the current General Director and President of the Board of Directors (the interviewee). The Director considers himself foremost an employee of the bank, rather than the leader of FoodCo.

Many of FoodCo.'s managers were fired, and the company basically ceased all operations. They are now primarily a holding company and provide some accounting services for the five strong subsidiaries of FoodCo., of which they own 80 to 90 percent of shares. The interviewee said that FoodCo. exists because the bank cannot monitor these subsidiaries itself. Their current business strategy consists of a plan to sell off all weak subsidiaries and gain increased control over those that are strong. These subsidiaries contribute a portion of their profits to repay debts that FoodCo. owes to the state foreign trading bank. The bank also plans to sell much of FoodCo.'s sizable and attractive property, located in a desirable section of Prague, once they feel the real estate market has reached its apex.

Thus, the managers gained autonomy as a result of a lack of concentrated or active ownership. But instead of using this situation to maintain control without the risks of ownership, or to reward themselves with high salaries and prestige, as Szelenyi's managerialism thesis (1995) suggests, the managers used this opportunity to steal huge amounts of money from FoodCo., much of which went into new private businesses.

The managerialism thesis cautions us not to focus too much on "petty thefts," and to focus on control rather than ownership. The unaccounted-for 4.5 billion crowns (about $173,000,000 USD), however, cannot be considered "petty theft." FoodCo.'s case belies Szelenyi's advice, and comes far closer to Staniszkis' theory of political capitalism, through which managers "spontaneously" privatize state assets. It should be emphasized, moreover, that FoodCo. is a Czech company. The Czech Republic, according to the latest formulation of the political capitalism thesis, was the only postcommunist country not to fall victim to this "kleptocratura" (Frydman, Murphy and Rapaczynski 1996).

The existence of enterprises whose managers form permanent satellite firms to suck profit from a large host firm is probably one of the unique features of postcommunist economic organizations. There are no current data on the pervasiveness of this type of activity. However, according to unpublished data from the Ministry of Trade and Industry, 40 percent of state enterprises in industry, trade and construction have founded several hundred of these "satellite" companies, using an average of 10 percent of their assets, as of mid-1990 (Earle, Frydman, and Rapaczynski 1993: 132).

This type of private company has been referred to in Eastern Europe as a "by-pass" or "tunneling" company. Managers employ such satellite strategies during a period of radical uncertainty prior to privatization, or in the absence of effective monitoring following a privatization. The self-seeking nature of humans, as emphasized by principal-agent theory (Demsetz 1988; Alchian and Demsetz 1972; Fama and Jensen 1983a and 1983b), seems to flourish in this situation. In essence, the "agents" are left unsupervised and unmonitored.

Aside from utilizing satellite strategies, actors can also draw on clientelistic financial networks to obtain the capital needed to privatize state property. This strategy involves employing a network of people that was formed in the socialist period. This network uses the power held by members in banks and other financials to issue loans to companies owned by members of the network. The members then typically use the loan to purchase shares of other companies. This practice can be both legal and illegal.

The acquisition of financial capital via clientelistic ties can occur via both legal and illegal means. For example, one large Hungarian factory in the sample of case studies was privatized by a limited liability company consisting of private Hungarian citizens. They paid for this privatization with an E-loan of 450 HUF ($3.46 million). (An E-loan is a special subsidized loan to be used for privatization, typically set at one-third to one-fourth the general interest rate.) By Hungarian law, a private person should have 150 percent of the value of the loan as collateral. In this case, my interviewee pointed out, no private person in the socialist period could have had the necessary private wealth to qualify for the loan. In fact, the loan was approved without the establishment of the existence of this collateral. As it turned out, one of the owners of the limited liability company was also a member of the Board of Directors of the bank issuing the E-loan.

A more legal, but no less impressive, example of this strategy was the establishment of GoldenGroup in the Czech Republic. This financial holding company was established in 1992 as a brokerage house and did investment banking for three years. The brokerage forms the heart of the company, and has acquired the other firms currently in the group. In the spring of 1995 it was changed into a holding company, which I will call GoldenGroup, and which lists among the top ten brokerage houses and asset managers in the Czech Republic. It includes the most important investment fund for the second wave of voucher privatization, as well as two investment funds from the first wave.[3] GoldenGroup owns an insurance company with 300,000 subscribers as well. The total assets of the group consist of 10 billion crowns (about $333,000,000 USD) and shares in over 70 companies.

GoldenGroup is fully private. Ninety-nine percent of its shares are in the hands of the top two managers—94 percent with the 32-year-old CEO and founder. The founder secured money for his firm's expansion as a result of cooperating with two banks. In one, GoldenGroup is the majority owner. In the other, GoldenGroup is a significant share owner. After the initial infusion of cash, the group grew rich trading in securities and buying vouchers during two waves of privatization. The initial money used to purchase shares in the group's two banks came from contacts the owner/CEO made while working in two state-majority-owned banks.

Obviously this strategy, like most others, is employed when it can be. That is, only the lucky few with connections to those who run or influence postcommunist financial institutions can employ this strategy.

Financial networks are not the only arena where clientelistic ties are useful. Network ties to members with political power can also be exercised. Actors use their ties to incumbents in positions of political authority to (a) gain appointments to positions as managers and as members of boards of directors; (b) demand the sale of shares of a company to a client; and (c) procure large and lucrative contracts from the state. They can then return some profits to those with political authority to further their political careers.

Political capitalism exists in all capitalist systems. Its prevalence, however, varies greatly among different postcommunist societies. In general, where democratic structures are strongest, and in particular where a free press is firmly entrenched, this strategy will be less prevalent. A transparent political system, in which the mass of the citizenry can find out what is going on and hold political actors accountable for their actions, will limit this process. Similarly, elite reproduction creates more potential network ties that can be mobilized for clientelistic strategies. Thus, where the technocracy, managers, and dissident intellectuals defeated the political bureaucracy during the transition from socialism, this process remains more limited. In the countries where the old political guard never lost power to an internal foe, but rather abandoned Communism as a result of external pressures, we find the greatest amount of political capitalism. Consequently, this strategy is comparatively rare in Hungary and the Czech Republic and more prevalent in Slovakia. It is much more typical of Eastern Europe and the Balkans than of Central Europe (it is found the most in Serbia, Bulgaria, Romania, and Russia).

Nonetheless, it does exist even in Hungary and the Czech Republic. In the Czech Republic, Klaus was forced to resign due to revelations of this type of activity. Similarly, according to an interviewee at the Hungarian State Property Agency and Holding Company, politicians try to exert pressure for the appointment to various boards of the five biggest corporations, and one hears that someone has been fired and replaced as a manager for political reasons approximately once a month.

My research found some evidence of "political capitalism" as well. The owner of a private consulting firm, founded in 1990 to provide services related to privatization, reported that after the last election in Hungary, they lost their contact on the board of the state property agency. Subsequently, they have not received any more contracts. They must now rely on helping local governments privatize their infrastructure. The firm, with a maximum of ten employees, had total sales of 70 million HUF prior to the election of the Socialists in 1994. By 1995 sales had fallen to only 14 million HUF. The rate of profit fell from the

40–60 percent range from 1990 to 1994, to 30 percent last year, and in 1996 the company showed only losses.

These varied strategies of managers are not all mutually exclusive. Managers of old socialist firms or new private enterprises can combine these different strategies in a number of ways which depend on the particular situation. For example, managers may use clientelistic access to bank loans in order to pursue a strategy of auto-cross-ownership, as discussed in the following section.

STRATEGIES RELYING ON MANAGERIAL AND EMPLOYEE OWNERSHIP

A straightforward alternative way to create domestic owners without recourse to clientelistic networks and satellite companies is a manager and/or employee buyout. This is a strategy in which a group of managers, often with the cooperation of workers, privatizes the original state-owned enterprise (or a division of such an enterprise). This is typically accomplished by forming a limited liability company that privatizes the original company, often on very favorable terms. It seems that cheap management buyouts may be used by the state as a way to prevent bankruptcies and save jobs. Thus, the resources used to employ this strategy are the political power of workers and managers, as well as the personal savings of firm insiders and/or the firm's cash reserves, which can be used to purchase the company.

Whether this practice takes the form of a manager and employee buyout, or simply an employee buyout, all commentators and researchers report (or assert) that managers then go on to dominate the new "employee-owners." First, the opportunity to subscribe to shares is often based on seniority and salary, which favors management (Karsai and Write 1994: 1005). And if seniority is not the principle of share distribution, then money is, which obviously also favors management. Furthermore, diffuse ownership among employees, as well as managerial monopolization of information, again, according to fairly preliminary data, further strengthen managers' position relative to workers.

Thus in Hungary,

Employee-Owners were typically, because of their low and diffuse equity stakes together with lack of expertise, unable to exercise an effective supervisory role. Moreover, employees were presented with insufficient information with which to exercise control, either in terms of proper representation or a system of weekly and monthly reports. Feasibility studies and business plans were neither detailed nor concrete enough to make these documents suitable for exerting some sort of external control. (Karsai and Write 1994: 1007)

Indeed, employees, "with their generally low equity stakes, did not see themselves as owners. As the proportion of their incomes made up by dividends was insignificant, the focus of employees' attention was on receiving higher wages and keeping their jobs" (Karsai and Write 1994: 1007). These findings are based on case studies of 17 firms, which is more evidence, to my knowledge, than anyone else has mustered on this point.

My own fieldwork also confirmed this view. In one Czech company, the CEO told me that the managers completely dominated the legally mandated process by which workers appoint one-third of the seats on the Supervisory Board. Similarly, the Chief Economists of the Hungarian State Property Agency told me that it was "common knowledge" that managers dominated employee buy-outs. Moreover, I found that over time managers tend to buy shares from employees. This was the case of five firms which I studied in Slovenia—where the privatization law mandated that insiders receive 60 percent of their firms' shares at privatization.

A related strategy relies on the fact that managers need not buy a majority stake in their firms to maintain control. Instead, they can purchase a minority block of shares, in order to fragment outside owners and ensure their own domination. This strategy allows management to gather a sufficient number of votes on the Board of Directors and/or the Supervisory Board to block a combination of non-management (outside) owners from gaining control of the corporation. A typical mechanism consists of managers creating a company that then purchases some shares of the firm in which the managers work. It is clear that this strategy increases the control of managers. By creating another "owner" with voting shares on the Supervisory Board, a partially self-owned firm can ensure that "outside" owners cannot gain the simple or two-thirds majority necessary to appoint the chairman of the Board of Directors. Managerial control is thereby secured, since Supervisory Boards are typically mandated by law to have one-third of their members be representatives of "employees." This term includes both managers and workers, but, as argued previously, usually refers to managers. Thus, these additional "self-owned" votes, combined with the one-third of the members that are representatives of employees, allows the management to block any move by outside owners.

One example of this found in my fieldwork involves CzechPress, a new company founded in 1994. CzechPress is a private alternative to the Czech state-run press agency (a local version of the Associated Press). The ownership and control of this company are very complicated. It is owned by seven companies. Six are investment funds (which in turn are owned by larger investment funds, which are owned by banks, which are majority-owned by the state) and one is a publisher. They have two main owners: GoldenGroup (of the previous example), which owns 35 percent, and the InvestGroup, which owns 34 percent. The Supervisory Board, which appoints the Board of Directors, has proportionate representation from the owners. There is no majority from one firm. As a twist in this ownership scenario, the top six managers of CzechPress, who also founded the company, own 90 percent of InvestGroup. Therefore they become one of their own major owners. My interviewee (the Chairman of the Board and Managing Director for the economic division) said that the managers control the firm because the owners are divided. At any rate, they own one of their own major owners.

The media division is run by the editor-in-chief. The economics division is headed by the director of the firm. The only way to remove either of them is through the Supervisory Board. The Supervisory Board consists of nine members, with a mandatory three from the employees and six from the shareholders. However, the three employee-appointed members, along with the representatives of the managers' own company, can always block any Supervisory Board action, since any decision requires agreement by two-thirds of the Supervisory Board. The interviewee said that "the company is completely run by the managers." These other owners were brought in simply to gain additional money for investments.

Like many new private firms, this firm was created by former dissidents and technocrats. Of the six managers who formed the investment fund that secures insider control of CzechPress, two were journalists, one worked in the financial sector selling bonds and shares, one was an election consultant, and one was a computer programmer who worked on over-the-counter stock-selling. The majority were mathematicians and physicists—they changed jobs after the revolution. Before the revolution they all had problems getting jobs for political reasons. After the revolution, because of their education, they were quickly able to learn the new economic laws and the functioning of the new capital market. They pooled the money they made at their new professions (two million crowns, about $67,000) and made six million crowns profit on the stock market in nine months, as they sold their holdings just when the market peaked. They took this money and started the investment company in order to open up CzechPress. These are the very actors described by Szelenyi in his managerialism thesis. However, they are not trying to blur property rights so much as to use very clear and precise property rights to their advantage.

This strategy seems to be possible when a firm is owned by more than several institutional owners. I saw only two examples of this out of the 50 firms I studied, both in the Czech Republic. As a result of the voucher privatization in this country, and the subsequent formation of investment funds which then purchased a majority of the privatized companies, many companies were owned by large institutional investors whose monitoring capacities were stretched quite thin. This would seem the ideal environment for this type of strategy. However, the dense network of interfirm holdings that Stark (1996) describes for the largest firms in Hungary would probably also be a fertile ground for this strategy.

Another form of self-ownership, certainly the most unusual and perhaps the most important type, is what I call auto-cross-ownership. Managers, using institutional power derived from their incumbency as managers, institutionally purchase other companies in a strategy of reciprocal cross-institutional ownership. These lines of cross-ownership are reinforced through interlocking Boards of Directors and Supervisory Boards. Thus, the primary resources used by managers employing this strategy are the interfirm networks formed during the socialist period and internal cash reserves.

This strategy creates an auto-cross-owned business group that perhaps can be called "the Czech Business Group." This organization is built around networks of managers in privately owned firms (consisting of firms in some manufacturing sector, along with affiliated companies that provide services, including banks, investment companies, and insurance companies). The most important real property rights of any group of concrete actors associated with the Czech Business Group are exercised by the top managers of these firms, with a network of power emanating from the Board of Directors and the Supervisory Board of the central "holding company."

These networks of firms are both "private" (to the extent that they are not owned by any organs of the state) and "self-owned." The resulting "networks of firms" resemble Japanese *keretsu*, or to a lesser extent Korean *Chaebol*. (See Stark and Bruszt [1995] for a similar finding, although one that focuses more attention on the role of continued state ownership of large banks.) The chief specificity of the Czech Group is that it is controlled by its top managers. There are no "ultimate private interests," with ownership based on the collective ownership of a large amount of capital and wealth by an extended family, as in the Korean and Japanese enterprises (see Zeitlin 1974; Zeitlin and Ratcliff 1988; Domhoff 1986). Hard as it may seem to understand, this is a non-state-owned property form without any significant "natural individuals" as shareholders. This goes beyond the managerialist claim that diffuse ownership by individual shareholders creates a situation in which managers control the corporation. There are no individual "shareholders" to speak of. The shareholders are the companies in the group. Some *keretsu* self-owned up to 80 percent of the shares in the companies in their group—this is the closest empirical phenomenon to the example of MegaChem.

This strategy can be pursued under only certain conditions. First, a peculiar legal and institutional structure must be in place. In particular, a large company must be formally owned by many smaller companies. This is most likely a largely contingent historical outcome. Second, the mother holding company must have a substantial amount of money, or access to financial institutions, in order to purchase the owning companies.

This property form might become increasingly dominant in the Czech Republic as the existing firms quickly grow, often incorporating and transforming firms with other organizational structures.[4] The so called "Third Wave of Privatization" is likely to create more Czech Business Groups as investment funds sort out and concentrate their ownership.[5] One of the investment experts from the firm that started the third wave of privatization explained the process to me.

He explained that his company (with funds from two banks that it bought) conducts "raids" on some of the big investment funds by purchasing them through hostile takeovers. His firm then scrutinizes their portfolio of firms and decides which firms to keep and actively manage, and which to sell off. He reported that this decision was based on the opportunities to combine firm assets. GoldenGroup also claimed to employ this strategy while sifting through their portfolio to decide over which firms in their vast holdings to consolidate control.

A case study of auto-cross-ownership involves MegaChem from the Czech Republic. The MegaChem group, the second-largest enterprise in the Czech Republic, trails only the state-owned electricity monopoly in terms of economic importance. Moreover, it is one of the only postcommunist multinational corporations with subsidiaries in over 20 companies located around the world. Depending on what it owns on any given day, according to the manager in charge of human resources, the group has about 10,000 employees.[6] The annual turnover of the group amounts to about 30 billion crowns, or about 1 billion U.S. dollars.

The transformation of MegaChem has been a big topic in the Czech press. My information on this group comes from press reports and interviews with one or more people who are (1) on the Board of Directors of MegaChem Group, (2) on the Supervisory Board of the MegaChem Group, (3) Executive Directors of companies within the group, (4) other top managers within the group, (5) Members of Boards of Directors and Supervisory Boards, as well as General Directors of Subsidiary companies (in which the group owns more than 50 percent of shares), or (6) members of Boards of Directors, Supervisory Boards, and General Directors of affiliated companies (in which MegaChem owns a significant, but not a majority, of shares). I also utilized internal documents, provided by the company, which detailed the ownership structure, as well as company annual reports. Finally, this material was supplemented with information available at the firm registry established to aid citizens/investors by providing information about companies.

MegaChem was founded in 1948 as the state-owned foreign trading company with a legal monopoly on all imports and exports of chemicals, pharmaceuticals, and petrochemical-related products. In 1968, along with a number of other trading companies, it was converted into a "corporatized" firm, or a "normal limited shareholding company." This meant that shares of MegaChem were formally owned by the firms whose products they traded. Thus, MegaChem was owned by the refineries, chemical industry firms, and pharmaceutical industry firms in Czechoslovakia, as well as the state foreign trade bank that made loans for exports and imports.

These firms did not have to pay for these shares, and in fact did not exercise any control rights. Similar to virtually all other firms in Czechoslovakia, MegaChem was controlled by a state ministry. The change in ownership was probably prompted by efforts to legitimize the regime with "reforms," rather than any economic logic. According to one of the interviewees, another reason for the change was that the Western firms with which MegaChem had contact as a trading company understood the meaning of a "joint-stock company." Thus, the formal change in ownership was an effort to smooth interaction with Western companies.

The structure of ownership of MegaChem has remained unchanged from 1968 until this day. Over 100 companies owned, and still own, MegaChem. In addition, about 4.5 percent of MegaChem's shares are owned by employees (mostly managers). After 1989, these owning companies were forced to pay for their shares, creating a huge source of cash for MegaChem. Many of these companies, once forced to trade through MegaChem in the Communist period, now attempted to eliminate the middleman and do their own marketing and distribution. These companies discovered, however, that this was not such an easy task.[7]

MegaChem had a distribution network already set up, and the "transaction costs" of establishing their own networks proved to be much higher than many firms expected. This problem, combined with the severe "transitional recession" that rocked the Czech Republic after the destruction of the COMECON trading block, created major problems for most firms in this sector. The President of MegaChem USA worked for one such company until 1993. He said that his company, like many in the sector, borrowed money from MegaChem equal to the value of their capital stock. Then, when the privatization process began, MegaChem made a debt-for-equity swap and acquired ownership of the company. In fact, MegaChem acquired a controlling interest in many firms in the sector. According to my interviewee, they were able to acquire over 50 percent of shares in most cases. In cases where MegaChem doesn't own over 50 percent of the shares, it can still exercise control by collaborating with other shareholders. In particular, MegaChem has a reciprocity-based working arrangement with a large, and quite famous, private institutional investor who votes with MegaChem to ensure MegaChem's control of these companies, in return for MegaChem's help in other sectors.

In June 1994, MegaChem formed a holding company, MegaChem Group, with ownership in over 60 different firms. The old MegaChem is now just one company (albeit the largest and most important) in this group. Firms in this group are mostly privatized firms in the petrochemical, chemical, and pharmaceutical industries. However, the group also includes an airline, hotel, printing company, and several professional sports teams, as well as significant banks, pension funds and investment funds.

These investment funds themselves own shares in some of these companies, further strengthening MegaChem's control over the sector. MegaChem frequently places members from their Boards of Directors on the Supervisory Boards of other firms, thus reinforcing their control. For example, the Chairman of the Board of Directors of the Czech-based pharmaceutical producer, which is one of the largest owners of MegaChem (which has not been privatized yet for political reasons[8]), is the Chairman of the Supervisory Board of MegaChem, just as the Chairman of the Board of Directors of MegaChem Group is the Chairman of the Supervisory Board of that pharmaceutical company. Obviously, interlocking directorates are being used as a way to link businesses.

Thus, MegaChem privatized its own owners, a process once referred to by a member of parliament as privatization by incest. Not only is ownership dispersed, but it is literally an example of self-ownership. Table 2.2 details this ownership structure.

Table 2.2
Major Owners of MegaChem

Organization	Percentage they own	Percentage owned by MegaChem
Czech Petroleum Products	11%	5–10%
Foreign Trading Bank	10%	1%
Slovak Chemical producer	6%	2–7%
Auto-owned	4.5%	NA
Oil Refinery	4%	25%
Czech Chemical producer	2–4%	20%
Czech Pharmaceutical	2–4%	none: not yet privatized
Czech motorfuels	2–4%	NA
Czech Rubber company	2–4%	NA
Subtotal	43–51%	53–63%

Source: Internal company documents and interviews.

The remaining ownership of MegaChem consists of very small ownership shares by tens of companies, in which MegaChem typically owns a controlling interest. MegaChem also owns several investment companies, which, in turn, own shares in some of the firms listed above, along with the smaller owners.

In the fall of 1995, MegaChem moved to further solidify control of the industrial group through an inner core of top management by buying back shares owned by employees (including the shares of managers and some enterprise directors). Throughout the Communist period, MegaChem had circumvented very strict wage controls by granting shares to some of its employees. The number of shares held increased as an employee moved to a higher position in the firm. Once wage controls were eliminated this was no longer necessary. In addition, according to the interviewees, the Board of Directors did not want employees potentially blocking any decisions. So they offered to pay one-and-a-half to two times the value of the stock in a buyback plan. The Board had also decided to increase MegaChem's basic capital by a factor of four and to eliminate dividends for the next few years. Thus, if an employee wanted to retain their stock they would have to pay the company four times its face value, receive no remuneration in the medium term, and forgo significant amounts of immediate money. This policy resulted in a complete buyback of the employee-owned stocks. Now a group of top managers owns these stocks, obviously solidifying their power.

Thus, MegaChem is a self-institutionally owned holding company with many subsidiaries, which cooperate with each other to maximize profits. The companies within this network of firms are controlled by the center, which is itself controlled by the top management of the holding company as well as the top management of other major firms in the group. The relationship between firms in the group was described to me as "regulated competition." The individual firms definitely coordinate their activities and give preferential treatment to firms within the group when selecting business partners. Indeed, this is even stated quite clearly within the annual report. Thus, the structure of MegaChem serves to reduce all kinds of transaction costs and potential market failures (see Williamson 1975, 1981).

If, however, one of the firms performs poorly, it can theoretically be replaced with a firm outside the group. If a company delivers overpriced or inferior goods, for example, it can be replaced as a supplier of inputs by another company. More importantly from the perspective of budget constraints, the interviewees all claimed that, after a few years, any firms in the group that are not profitable will be allowed to go bankrupt. It remains to be seen if this is true. Finally, according to one of the interviewees, the transactions of firms within the group are arranged to minimize taxation through the well-known multinational strategy of "transfer pricing." This is a process in which commodities sold between subsidiaries of the same MNC have set prices that minimize "profits" in subsidiaries with already high profits, thus reducing the total tax bill.

MODIFYING EXISTING SOCIOLOGICAL ACCOUNTS OF THE PROCESS OF POSTCOMMUNIST TRANSFORMATION

These findings, the identification of the various strategies and combinations of strategies employed by postcommunist economic elites to transform the postcommunist economy, do not completely corroborate the reigning interpretations of economic transformation in the postcommunist world.

Nee's market transition theory doesn't tell us very much about the emergence of capitalism in Eastern Europe—very few of the firms in my sample grew out of the socialist second economy. Clearly, former economic elites had a massive advantage in the creation of new firms. I saw nothing resembling the "marketized firm" Nee described in China. While local governments did own an important share of some businesses, I detected none of the kind of "local state corporatism" observed in Chinese townships. Eastern European capitalism is not emerging from below, as in China, but remains a top-down process.

Stark's recombinant property theory provides the greatest insight into the process of transformation in Eastern Europe. Each strategy can be seen as a recombination of various assets—political, clientelistic, business connections, and so forth. Primarily, the ability of economic elites to draw on informal networks allows for the successful appropriation of ownership and/or control of postcommunist firms.

Conversely, the extent of recombinant property, as described by Stark's Heavy Metal case study, is not overwhelming. In fact, I saw no enterprises that fit this model. I did observe some "network" production, but these did not involve a series of satellites operating around a mother firm. Rather, this network production was more like the straightforward vertical integration so prevalent in capitalist economies, in which a firm expands upstream and downstream on the commodity chain. In the Czech Republic, the MegaChem example of auto-cross-ownership seems very similar to recombinant property—with one major modification. This firm is almost wholly private. In Stark's Heavy Metal example, the state owned the holding company that owned the subsidiaries. In the case of MegaChem, there is no actual state ownership. Instead, a small amount of state involvement occurs by virtue of the fact that one of the owners of MegaChem is a bank which is itself partially owned by the state. Thus, the fundamental insight that this is "neither public nor private property" is contradicted. A more precise definition, I think, would describe recombinant property as a combination of a strategy of creating parasitic satellites (thus the privatizing of assets and the centralizing liabilities) and a strategy of auto-cross-ownership, along with a continuation of state ownership. As such, it is very likely to be a transitory type of property. That is, many firms in "recombinant" ownership may be privatized piece by piece.

Of course, Heavy Metal is a real example, and thus some recombinant property definitely exists in Eastern Europe. Stark, however, claims not only that this type of property exists, but also that it is the dominant form in Hungary. Stark cites as primary evidence the fact that about 18 percent of the 220 largest enterprises and banks were institutionally owned as of 1993.

According to my survey data, however, only 8.7 percent of the 3000 largest firms in Hungary are majority institutionally owned. This does not, moreover, mean that 8.7 percent of the 3000 largest firms are examples of recombinant property as defined by Stark. It is quite possible that several companies may be owned by a company that is 100 percent privately owned, and thus may also show up as a case of "inter-enterprise ownership." An example of this is found in my case study of a Hungarian agribusiness with approximately 300 employees. This company was founded in 1990 with one million forints. Now it boasts an annual turnover of more than two billion forints and owns 100 percent of five companies that take part in a vertically integrated network of production. However, these firms weren't part of a "Recombinet" combining public and private property, since all companies are, directly or indirectly, privately owned by the director/founder and his daughter. Once again, I observed a tight connection between ownership and control in a Hungarian firm. Just as importantly, I observed a clarification of property rights rather than a blurring of them.

The owner of this agribusiness started his company by buying a German license to produce all types of animal food. He currently controls eight percent of the Hungarian market, and, among eight nationwide producers, is the fourth largest (the first two are American multinational companies, the third a Hungarian firm). There are also many regional and local producers. Through privatization, his company bought a plant that produces animal food to increase their capacity. He also formed a company which produces the machines that make the animal food.

He has recently started expanding upstream and downstream from his foothold in the poultry-feed business. With the direct cooperation of a Dutch firm, he started a company that raises parent-stock. He pays farmers to raise chickens with his parent-stock and provides them with chicken feed. He has an arrangement with two slaughterhouses to sell each of them 1.5 million chickens a year. In addition, although he still plans to provide chickens to the other slaughterhouses, he is constructing two slaughterhouses of his own. He has also formed a company to sell the poultry that he slaughters.

All the companies mentioned are owned entirely by his company, which is owned entirely by him and his daughter. He is transforming his original company into a holding company that will control all the others. He plans on keeping 60 percent of the shares of all these companies in the holding company, and selling the other 40 percent to small investors. He said he would not sell to large investors as he is determined to keep control of these companies himself. In this group of companies, all but the holding company owned by him and his daughter would show up statistically as "interenterprise ownership," but this is clearly not what Stark means by "recombinant property." Thus, while "recombinant property" certainly exists, as in Stark's well-documented case study of Heavy Metal, it does not represent the dominant new form of property in Hungary, as Stark believed.

Some available data provide a more precise measure of the pervasiveness of recombinant property than "institutional ownership." Table 2.3 measures the extent of recombinant ownership patterns among a mail survey that sampled the 3000 largest Hungarian firms in 1995.

As can be seen from these data, recombinant ownership patterns, the cross-ownership of buyers and suppliers orbiting around a state-owned mother firm, although important, do not appear to comprise the "dominant" property form in Hungary.

Like Stark's recombinant property thesis, Szelenyi's managerialism thesis also finds some support from my case studies. Simple self-ownership and auto-cross-

Table 2.3
Percentage of Firms with "Recombinant" Ownership Patterns

Do the firm or managers own any shares in your:	Yes	Percent of all firms in sample
Buyers	10	6.9%
Suppliers	6	4.2%
Competitors	7	4.9%
Middlemen	11	7.6%
Subcontractors	8	5.6%

N = 144

Source: 1995 Hungarian mail survey of 600 randomly sampled firms from a list of the largest 3000 firms in 1993. One hundred fifty firms no longer existed in 1995, and of the remaining 450 firms, 144 surveys were completed for a response rate of 32 percent.

ownership strategies provide examples of managers gaining control of corporations without assuming all the risks of ownership. These managers can reward themselves with high salaries without risking all their assets by investing them into firms. The strategy of establishing parasitical satellites is an even more effective way for managers to reward themselves without risking ownership.

On the other hand, most self-ownership and auto-cross-ownership strategies do not seem to be motivated by a desire to avoid the risks of ownership. Rather, these strategies are employed when some group of managers, not having enough money to buy a controlling amount of shares in a company, still want all control rights of the firm. For this reason we find this strategy employed by managers from bigger firms.

Staniszkis' theory of political capitalism also found some confirmation in my fieldwork. The political capitalism strategy for gaining ownership certainly can be described as a conversion of political power into economic ownership. Of course, the pervasiveness of this strategy is determined primarily by political factors exogenous to the firm. This type of activity is tolerated at different levels in the different countries. In Slovakia, for example, it is common knowledge that some of the biggest enterprises are divided up among the political power holders, primarily Meciar and his clients (although the other parties are involved as well). Still, this process is only one among many, and it hardly characterizes the majority of property transformation in Hungary or the Czech Republic, and probably not in Slovakia either.

NOTES

1. David Stark pointed this out to me.

2. See Walters 1990; Nuti 1990; Mejstrik 1995: 56; Voska 1993: 106; Staniszkis 1991: 38–40.

3. "Voucher Funds" refer to investment companies that primarily purchase the citizen investment "vouchers" that all Czechs over 18 years of age had a right to buy for a small sum (about one-fifth of an average monthly salary). Each voucher certificate would have 1000 investment points with a book value of about 60,000 crowns ($2,000, which was closer to the average yearly wage). These voucher points could then be invested during rounds of bidding on many of the over 2,000 state-owned enterprises approved for privatization. There was little interest in the program, until investment companies were established that offered shares in their company in exchange for the privatization vouchers. After a year they promised to buy back the shares for ten to fifteen times what the person paid for them. This was too good a deal for most Czechs to pass up, as 82 percent of adults participated. Of the 5.95 million vouchers, 72.2 percent went to these funds, and the rest were invested by individuals (see Mertlik 1996: 59).

4. Of course, this form of property can only exist if it is deemed legal by political authority. It is also possible that some group of politically connected individuals will eventually attempt to gain controlling shares of the entire business group. Thus, auto-cross-ownership could be a "transitional" form of property.

5. The first two "waves of privatization" refer to the two rounds of citizen-voucher privatization, as described above. The "third wave" refers to the unofficial process by which

investment funds, the recipients of about three-quarters of all the vouchers, sort the wheat from the chaff among their vast partial holdings. Thus, companies like GoldenGroup, owning stake in over 70 enterprises, must eventually decide which ones it wants to really administer and control, and which ones it may sell off.

6. MegaChem group is actively participating in the "third wave of privatization." Thus, what it "owns" fluctuates on a daily basis.

7. This contrasts with the situation in the food sector we observed at FoodCo.; probably due to the different nature of the two groups of commodities. Chemicals and pharmaceuticals must be of very high quality and purity. While foodstuffs must also be fresh, it is extremely easy to tell if they are not up to standards—they stink. Chemicals and pharmaceuticals, however, require expensive testing to ensure their quality. Thus, there is a much greater need for trust in the network of suppliers and consumers. As trust comes with repeated business transactions, an advantage is gained by the old monopoly trading house which has been in existence for a long time.

8. This company is the major producer of generic medicines in the Czech Republic. Because the health system is in a bit of disarray, the government is reluctant to privatize this company before elections, for fear that it might be bought by foreign companies. Because the company is the market's major supplier of cheap pharmaceuticals, the sale to foreign capital could provide an opening for political attacks by the opposition.

3

The Structure of Capitalism in Eastern Europe

The aforementioned account of the different strategies that managers employed to create capitalism suggests that Eastern European economies are mixed social formations. The existing accounts of the transition reviewed in the first chapter focus narrowly on one type of firm, with one set of property rights, and then generalize to the entire economy. They fail to stress the heterogeneity of property forms in the new economies of postcommunist Eastern Europe.

A THEORY OF POSTCOMMUNIST CAPITALISM

In spite of the diversity of organizational forms emerging from the multiple strategies of transition employed by strategically located actors, I would like to offer a theory of postcommunist capitalism which states that these mixed systems are dominated by the activity of market-dependent firms which are "private" to the extent that they are non-state, and which, in addition to market integration, face two specifically Eastern European forms of economic integration: subterranean redistribution and the clientelistic allocation of financial capital.

The dominant form of property is "private" in the sense that a majority of firms are not owned by the state. Table 3.1 shows the ownership structure of Hungarian and Czech industry in 1993.

In 1993, the biggest single majority owners of large businesses in Hungary was still the state. Stark and Bruszt (1995) claim that in the Czech Republic the state owns a far larger share of the economy than the data in Table 3.1 would indicate. This is because many private businesses are owned by investment companies that

Table 3.1
The Ownership Structure of the Hungarian and Czech Economies in 1993

Majority Ownership by	Hungarian Firms (N = 1001)	Hungarian Industry (N = 404)	Czech Industry (N = 257)
State	38.3%	40.1%	26.3%
Foreign	14.1%	17.6%	5.6%
Domestic Institutional	8.7%	8.2%	NA
Domestic Individual	10.9%	7.2%	8.2%
All Private[1]	19.6%	15.4%	22.5%
Majority Manager- and Employee-owned	11.6%	13.1%	30.7%

Source: Hungarian data are based on interviews with directors of a sample of 1001 firms out of the largest 3000 companies in Hungary (of which 404 are industrial). Czech data come from a mail survey of a random sample of 257 firms (returned from a questionnaire sent to 1000 of the 3000 largest industrial firms in the Czech Republic). The firms returning the questionnaire were not significantly different from the entire sample. The Czech data come from Zemplinerova, Lastovicka and Marcincin 1995.

are owned by investment funds that are, in turn, controlled by the major banks, which are still significantly owned by the state.[2]

However, according to my research, the actual property rights of the state are much less than these statistics would indicate. The "content" of state ownership, in most cases, is nothing more than the ability to prevent the sale of a firm. According to my interviewees, the "state's" behavior as an owner functions either to (1) maximize profits or (2) privatize the rest of their property as soon as possible. Both imperatives stem from trying to maximize state revenues and minimize state expenditures.

Furthermore, the notion that the state has the capacity to exercise control rights is somewhat suspect. According to interviews I conducted with people in the Hungarian State Privatization and Holding Company, each case officer oversees 15 firms and hardly has the capacity to exercise control of these firms. The firm managers simply have a near monopoly of information. Therefore, according to my interviewees, very little is done against the will of the managers. In the Czech Republic, it seems very unlikely that the state can actually exercise its property rights in any systematic way through the long chain of ownership that runs from the state to the banks to the investment funds to the investment companies to the actual enterprises. According to my interviewees, the investment companies primarily acted as absentee owners, pushing firms to increase dividends to the exclusion of all other goals. In this respect, Czech investment companies behaved in a manner reminiscent of the Hungarian state (see confirming studies in Rona-Tas 1996; Kenway and Klacova 1996).

As a result of the strategies employed by economic elites, a majority of the property in Eastern Europe is now, or will soon be, "private." This means that the rights of ownership—the right to take residual profits, the right to control and organize production, and the right to sell the property—are mostly with "non-state" actors. While all of these rights are limited by various laws, as in the advanced capitalist economies, they still fundamentally reside outside the sphere of the state and are carried out primarily by the owners or the managers of businesses. The most attenuated of these rights remains the right to transfer ownership. Because of the still-large amount of formal state ownership, the sale of assets remains, in these cases, outside the exclusive control of the "private owners" and firm insiders.

It is also important to emphasize that in Eastern Europe "private ownership" exists in varieties not found in the West. Most significantly, some "private owners" consist of auto-cross-owned firms. That is, the management of firms, or networks of management among a number of firms, consolidate their control over their enterprises, creating a situation where the "firm" as a legal entity owns itself.

Furthermore, at least in Hungary, there is no doubt that the state owns far less property now than it did in 1993 as a result of an additional three years of privatization activity and the growth of the private sector. According to the State Privatization and Holding Company, 1994 data from tax returns found that firms in the corporatized sector (which does not include government bureaucracies, schools or the army) had 58 percent of their total assets owned by private investors. Because of the privatization of the electricity sector and other activity, the 1995 estimate now shows that 70 percent of total assets in the corporatized sector reside in private hands.

The data in Table 3.2 support the argument that state ownership is in serious decline. The percentage of firms in which the state owned a majority of shares

Table 3.2
The Change in Property Forms from 1992 to 1996 in Hungarian Firms with at Least 50 Employees

At Least 25% Ownership by:	All firms 1992 (N = 640)	All firms 1995 (N = 293)
No category with 25%	5.5%	6.5%
State	43.9%	13.7%
Private Domestic	28.8%	52.2%
Foreign	13.6%	18.1%
State and Private Domestic	5.2%	4.8%
Foreign and Private	3.3%	4.8%

Source: 1996 data are based on a 1996 survey of 293 firms, randomly sampled from all firms with 50 employees or more by the professional social research firm Tarki. The 1992 data are from a 1993 Tarki survey of 1001 firms, sampled from the largest 3000 firms in 1993.

decreased enormously, while domestic ownership exploded. Foreign ownership also increased, although not nearly as much as domestic ownership.

Thus, the "typical" property form in Eastern European societies today has evolved into one of many types of "nonstate" (and thus "private") property. The fall in state ownership, and the subsequent rise in private ownership, is remarkable. There has been a smaller increase in foreign ownership, and all other forms have remained essentially unchanged.

THE FIRMS ARE MARKET-DEPENDENT

The vast majority of the firms I studied buy their inputs from other firms (they are not given to them by a central redistributor), and sell their output "on the market." That is, they enter into voluntary agreements with other parties, and are not told to whom or at what price to sell (see Kornai 1980). They must hire wage labor which is free to go to another job at any time. Their success comes from their profit, and their profit comes from maximizing revenue from the sale of commodities while minimizing the cost of producing these commodities. Other case studies conducted in Hungary and the Czech Republic also support these conclusions (Matesova 1993–94 and 1994; Hovanyi 1993–94; Belka et al. 1993; Capek and Mertlik 1996; Carlin, Von Reenen and Wolf 1995; Zemplinerova, Lastovicka and Marcincin 1995).

SUBTERRANEAN REDISTRIBUTION, POLITICAL CAPITALISM AND THE CLIENTELISTIC ALLOCATION OF BANK LOANS

For some of the firms in these economies, however, market-dependence is mitigated by three competing modes of economic integration. The first depends upon a political allocation of resources, the result of the successful employment of strategies involving political capitalism. The second involves the persistence of state redistribution of capital through a process I call "subterranean redistribution." It is "subterranean" because this redistribution is not advertised, in an attempt to hide it from the eyes of the West.

Instead of issuing subsidies to companies, the postcommunist state adopted less transparent means of softening budget constraints. Some of these methods include granting preferential credit rates, canceling debts, performing debt-for-equity swaps, and other methods. For example, in 1992 the Hungarian government selected 13 firms, "The Big Thirteen," that would be supported with an industrial policy. These firms were indebted to the state rather than to suppliers or banks. "The total asset value of the selected thirteen firms was assessed at nearly HUF 150 billion and their total debts at HUF 56 billion. (These figures do not include supplier credits in the range of another HUF 25 or 30 billion.) The [State

Owned Enterprises] involved more than 80 thousand employed people. Their turnover plan for 1992 was HUF 230 billion" (Voszka 1994: 67). In addition to these 13 firms, the Ministry of Industry and Trade reported that, in 1993, the debt of seven companies, worth 11.1 billion HUF, was canceled, rescheduled or swapped (68). "According to the report of the National Auditors, HUF 24 billion was underwritten by the [State property agency] by the end of 1992, and the amount doubled by mid-1993"(Voszka: 70).

In addition, the government has put informal pressure on banks to keep lending money (68). Then, in an attempt to strengthen the banking sector, which was saddled with bad debts, the government cleared bad debts of 102 billion forints and did an equity swap of another 80 billion. In 1993 the government did a debt consolidation for the banks of another 300 billion forints (70). This same year, an organization called the Underwriting Co. (in which the state has a majority interest) was founded to support the credit rating of private businesses which can promise high rates of return but do not have enough collateral to get loans from commercial banks. It guarantees up to 80 percent of loans (or HUF 100 million of commercial bank loans), and is backed by the Small Business Guarantee Fund, which is financed by the central government (70). This subtle form of redistribution is similar to the Export Guarantee Co. set up in 1991. If a firm can make payments on loans for financing raw materials and components for production, the state will issue the loans (71).

One strategy that may be pursued by new firms is to try to acquire some of this subterranean redistribution. For example, the Hungarian "clone company" described above that makes traffic lights and automated parking machines, received loans from the national Technological Development fund for their research and development; this is the only thing they invest in. The loans must be matched with income from profits. These loans sound like a subsidy; as the interviewee said, they have no interest payments and, in fact, "don't really have to pay them back." Indeed, bargaining with the state over taxes and loans somewhat mitigates the market-dependence of firms. One Hungarian interviewee said that "the state bank is like a tax agency, and the tax agency is like a state bank."

Subterranean redistribution might be a "transition strategy" for postcommunist governments (or even banks), and it may be discontinued or may have already disappeared. Table 3.3 summarizes evidence of subterranean redistribution in Hungary and the Czech Republic.

Much like in Hungary, the Czech government initially purchased 39 billion crowns worth of bad loans from banks. When this proved inadequate, the Consolidation Bank was created in 1991 to buy bad debt from banks. It took 110 billion crowns of "nonperforming" debt and an additional 15 billion crowns of "bad loans." In 1993 the state granted the bank another 15.7 billion crowns against bad loans. Privatization assets worth 23.7 billion crowns were used to relieve the debt of privatized firms by the end of 1993, with another 30.3 billion earmarked for debts incurred prior to 1991.

Table 3.3
Evidence of Subterranean Redistribution

	Czech Republic	*Hungary*
Legal barriers to bankruptcy	Yes	No
Government purchases bad loans from banks	178 billion Kc	402 billion Ft
Government assumes debt of specific firms	3 billion Kc	66 billion Ft
Government does debt for equity swap with banks	No	80 billion Ft
Government grants preferential credit or credit ratings	No	Yes
Privatization assets used to relieve enterprise debt	54 billion Kc	No
Informal pressure on banks to make loans	Yes	Yes

In Hungary the bank bailout took the form of 102 billion forints in the first bank consolidation program and 300 billion forints in the second bank consolidation program. The government provision of preferential credit took the form of the Underwriting Co. and the Export Guarantee Co., both funded by the central government.

Governments also mitigate market dependence by neglecting to enforce the bankruptcy laws that are in effect, or by so greatly watering them down that almost no firms go formally bankrupt. In Hungary in 1992 a harsh new bankruptcy law, *Law IL of 1991 on Bankruptcy Procedures, Liquidation Procedures and Final Settlement*, went into effect, replacing the old 1986 law. This law was supposed to function like the U.S. law that shields a firm from creditors to allow it to restructure and reorganize. A firm must file bankruptcy if it is more than 90 days behind in its payments. If the firm does not file, the managers become personally liable for any losses that result. One motivation for this law, aside from hoping to introduce hard-budget constraints, was to break the cycle of interenterprise debt that was vitiating the government's control over monetary policy.

This law resulted in a rash of bankruptcies. Between the time the law came into effect and July 1995, 3,167 enterprises filed for bankruptcy proceedings, or roughly 1.43 percent of total enterprises. Of these, 2,891 have carried out these proceedings. Fifty-one percent of them (1,490) have been liquidated. Another 45.5 percent (1,314) have reached agreements with their creditors, and 87 fall into the category of "other." Although I do not have figures with which to compare the liquidation rate, it seems particularly low considering that Hungary entered a "recession" more severe than the Great Depression in the United States. Moreover, according to the Minister of Industry, 40 to 45 percent of enterprises under state authority were facing bankruptcy at the time of the law's enactment (Earle, Frydman, and Rapaczynski 1993: 117). Thus, a very small number of firms that should have gone bankrupt, according to the laws of creative destruction, did so. More significantly, the rate of bankruptcy fell considerably after the first year of the new law. From December 1993 through June 1996, only 93 companies signaled their intention to pursue bankruptcy proceedings, a truly insignificant number. Although Hungary experienced a flood of bankruptcies, they quickly subsided. To date there have been very few bankruptcies in the Czech Republic.

The third type of economic activity articulating with market integration is the "clientelistic allocation of financial capital." That is, networks formed in the socialist period between managers of firms and managers in banks distribute much of the capital (how much, exactly, no one knows). My fieldwork uncovered several spectacular examples which have already been discussed, such as GoldenGroup and WoodCo. Interviewees from every firm, however, agreed that this did and does occur.

The example of clientelistic capitalism described above deals with a firm that benefited from this activity. It is quite possible, however, to get trapped on the wrong side of the bank-firm closure inherent in the clientelistic allocation of capital. In such circumstances, one firm subsidizes the loans of another, perhaps less creditworthy, company. LuxComp, a Czech trading company that imported certain luxury items during the Communist period, was one of these "losing" companies in the bank-firm interface.

LuxComp first became indebted during the transitional crisis following 1989. According to the General Director and Chairman of the Board of Directors, the old state foreign trade bank practices two types of parasitic behavior with respect to his firm.

LuxComp uses loans to staff its inventory. In order to get these loans, the bank pressures the firm to pay off some debt by selling their real estate at far below (10 to 20 percent) its market value. He stated that people in the bank with connections with realtors personally profit from this practice

The bank also seems committed to keeping the firm indebted and continually paying interest. From January 1993 to December 1995, the firm paid 50 percent of the principal of its debt. In addition, they paid interest in the last three years equal to their whole debt. The interest rate was an incredibly high 18.5 percent until it was lowered slightly to 15.35 percent in March of 1995. The bank schedules the firms' loan repayments so that the firm pays a maximum amount of interest.

This extraction is so severe that numerous joint ventures arranged by the director with various Western companies are starved of capital. The mechanism by which this extraction works is similar to the system of "debt-peonage" to which sharecroppers are subjected. On the last day of every month, the bank withdraws interest on LuxComp's debts, plunging them into debt again for the next month. Then they charge them a penalty on the bad debt. In this way, they take 32 percent in interest, almost twice the already extremely high rate. Thus, for the first 20 days of the month the firm is in debt. This debt slowly diminishes against the sales revenues, and a positive balance builds up by the end of the month. However, just before the closing statement, the bank again withdraws interest, and again plunges the firm into debt. Again the interest penalty is invoked and the cycle repeats. The interviewee pointed out that LuxComp's total assets are 1.2 billion crowns, and that their debts are only a quarter of this. Thus, what should be a relatively healthy firm is denied the capital it needs to diversify or expand business operations.

There is no doubt that both the clientelistic allocation of financial capital and subterranean redistribution are facilitated because the major state banks hold a large amount of bad debt among interdependent firms in the still highly monopolized postcommunist economy. This, in turn, gives them an incentive not to force widespread bankruptcies, since that could trigger a gale of "creative destruction" that could wipe out a significant number of firms (both profitable and unprofitable) in their portfolio, thereby destroying the bank.

Subterranean redistribution may create an environment ripe for the clientelistic allocation of capital because capital, by and large, does not go disproportionately to market-worthy firms. This strategy was also facilitated because the postcommunist banking sector lacked the monitoring capabilities needed to distinguish between well-run firms and inefficiently run firms. Thus, a loan to a member of a clientelistic network would not be very easy to spot. Therefore, I suggest that there is an elective affinity between subterranean redistribution and the clientelistic allocation of financial capital.

Tables 3.4 and 3.5 present evidence consistent with my suggestion that the best predictor of a firm receiving loans is bank or government ownership, rather than profitability or market performance. As shown in Table 3.4, the level of profitability in 1993 is in no way related to whether a firm received a loan in 1994. On the other hand, as Table 3.5 demonstrates, firms with bank or state ownership are much more likely to receive loans than firms without bank or state ownership. This relationship is statistically significant.

Table 3.4
Profitability and Access to Bank Loans

	Profitability in 1993		
	< 1%	1–10%	> 10%
No Bank loans 1994	15	15	7
Bank loans 1994	18	12	7

Table 3.5
Bank and State Ownership of Firms and Bank Credit

	No Bank or State Ownership	*Bank or State Ownership*
No Bank Loans	25	18
Bank Loans	10	28

Pearson Chi-Square = 8.32557 with 1 DF is significant at 0.00391

Source: 1995 Hungarian mail survey of 600 randomly sampled firms from a list of the largest 3000 firms in 1993. One hundred fifty firms no longer existed in 1995, and of the remaining 450 firms, 144 surveys were completed for an overall response rate of 32%. Of those 144, 83 completed a longer version of the questionnaire that contained questions on bank ownership and loans.

FUTURE ECONOMIC DEVELOPMENT AND STRUGGLE

When considering the possible developmental consequences of different types of property, one must realize that this is not a structurally determined process. The future of economic development in this region will be in part determined by the outcome of numerous struggles between different "fractions" or "segments" of the emergent dominant "postcommunist capitalist" class (or conflicts between different groups of the economic elite) and potentially interclass conflict as well (between employers and workers). (See Zeitlin 1984 and Brenner 1976 for this type of analysis in other contexts.) These class segments, I argue, will partly be based on different types of firms.

This struggle will take place on the political level, where different groups (at least partially based on different types of firms) will struggle for control of, and influence over, the state and the legal framework of property rights. One instrument of this will be the lobbying process, as well as overall influence on the election process. This struggle will also take place at the economic level, where different firms use their economic power to wage war on other firms, as, for example, through predatory takeovers or price wars. Eventually, as population ecologists suggest, some firms will be "selected" at the expense of other types of firms (Hannan 1989; Hannan and Freeman 1977). Of course, they might be selected on bases other than efficiency, such as access to political power, sources of investment, and so on.

NOTES

1. In the Czech republic this includes majority ownership by investment funds (8.5 percent) and individual voucher owners (5.8 percent).

2. These two samples are not exactly comparable because the Czech firms were sampled from a larger number of firms. Clearly, the largest 3000 industrial firms in the Czech sample are drawn from a pool of firms larger than the largest 3000 firms in the Hungarian sample, for the Hungarian population of firms includes many nonindustrial firms. Thus, the Czech sample probably contains more small firms, which are more likely to be subject to management and employee buy-outs. This would tend to reduce the level of state ownership relative to the Hungarian sample.

4

Manichean Economics: The Role of Foreign Capital in the Transition to Capitalism in Eastern Europe

In the second chapter of this book I identified various strategies employed by managers, technocrats and former political dissidents to transform socialist property and/or create new private firms in the postcommunist economies. One of the most important strategies I identified relied on joining forces with foreign capitalists. In this chapter I further analyze this strategy, demonstrating that there are, in fact, very different forms of foreign investment that must be analytically distinguished.

By attempting to desegregate various types of foreign investment, this analysis runs counter to most approaches to this topic. Indeed, few issues invoke such heated rhetoric or dogmatic analyses as the role of foreign capitalists, and especially foreign direct investment, in economic modernization and development. The fear and loathing inspired in some by the domination of an economy by ultra-exploitative multinational corporations are matched by the vigor with which the vast majority of mainstream economists celebrate the developmental virtues of such investment.

While images of effortless development via concessions to foreign investors juxtaposed to images of dangerous and abusive multinational juggernauts make for good polemics, they do not facilitate understanding of this vitally important phenomenon.

SOCIOLOGICAL ACCOUNTS OF THE ROLE OF FOREIGN CAPITAL IN TRANSFORMING NONCAPITALIST OR NONDEVELOPED SOCIETIES

It was not until the wave of decolonization following World War II that the effects of contact with the capitalist West on "noncapitalist" economies became an area of sociological inquiry. Prior to this, most social analyses focused on the issue of imperialism, emphasizing the effect that the interaction between capitalist and non-capitalist economies had on the political and economic conditions of the imperialist society.[1]

The first post–World War II school of thought to analyze the effects that contact with the capitalist or "advanced" West had on "noncapitalist" or traditional societies was modernization theory. While there are many different versions of modernization theory, they all seek to explain the process by which traditional societies are transformed into modern societies. Traditional and modern societies are ideal types, with the former implying backwardness, rural life and underdevelopment, and the latter implying modernity, urban life and industrialization. It is assumed that all societies will follow the same path as they move from "traditional" to "modern." Thus, modernization theorists believe that eventually the political, economic and social structures of nations in the "Third World" will come to resemble the structures of the nations of the "Advanced West."

Perhaps the father of contemporary modernization theory was Talcott Parsons. Certainly his influence was enormous in American sociology and political science departments. Parsons described five pattern variables. These pattern variables characterize either modern or traditional society and are binary opposites.

The first, *affective* behavior, occurs when actors seek immediate gratification. This contrasts with *affect neutrality*, in which behavior is instrumental for some ultimate goal. *Ascription* occurs when individual status is determined by ascribed characteristics, whereas in modern society, people are assigned status by their *achievement*. In traditional societies, relationships are *diffuse* and involve many unspecified dimensions simultaneously, such as kinship, economic and ethnic. In contrast, in modern societies people relate to each other in ways that are clear and delimited. In traditional societies, *particularism* exists when people relate to each other in specific ways, depending on the specific situation. In contrast, modern societies are characterized by *universal role expectations*, in which people act in accordance with objective rules of interaction.

Hoselitz (1965) directly borrows these variables from Parsons with minor variations to explain development in the Third World. Societies develop as they come to be characterized by the more "advanced" patterns of behavior, as they incorporate characteristics from the West as a result of continual contact. Occasionally, modernization theorists specify a particular agent in this transformation, often the "entrepreneur" with the "need for achievement." (See David McClelland's famous work on this topic [1964].)

The implication of Hoselitz's theory, as with all modernization theories, is that the greater the contact noncapitalist societies have with the Western nations, and the more they participate in the world markets, the more they will develop, either through a change in pattern variables or involvement in Western markets. Chenery and Eckstein (1970), for example, explicitly argue that foreign direct investment spurs development by providing capital unavailable from domestic sources, which, in the long run, make exports and import substitution industrialization possible, thereby reducing dependency.

Modernization theorists trumpeted the virtues of contact with the West for the "transitional" societies of the newly democratic and independent European colonies of Africa and Asia. The resulting lack of development and return to authoritarian rule (or even barbarism in some cases), combined with the anti-imperialist sentiment that accompanied the Vietnam War, essentially eliminated modernization theory from the academy.[2] Dependency Theory, the razor sharp rhetoric of A. G. Frank, and the historical breadth of Wallerstein and his world systems theory, quickly and almost completely eclipsed the Modernizationists.

In the absence of a strong sociology contingent to cry the victory of modernization theory with the fall of Communism, neoclassical economists have stood admirably in their place. While privatization is seen as the major tool in transforming these economies, this is not deemed sufficient. Foreign investment is often seen as a necessary compliment to privatization. First, FDI brings crucial Western knowledge and values in the form of superior Western management techniques, business ethics, entrepreneurial attitudes, labor intensity and production techniques. Second, FDI makes possible industrial upgrading by tying firms into global research and development networks and thus technology transfer, as well as by providing a great deal of investment capital. Third, FDI makes possible the growth of enterprises by providing access to crucial Western markets. This growth, in turn, provides a source of new jobs and stimulates demand for inputs from domestic suppliers. Fourth, FDI introduces new market entrants that reduce the monopolization of the recipient economy. (See Svetlicic, Artisien, and Rojec 1993: 10; Dunning 1993: 30; Hamar 1994: 188; Mann 1991: 184; Zloch-Christy 1995: 1; Csaki 1995: 108; Faur 1993: 204).

Many arguments closely mirror the imagery and logic of modernization theories. For example, "Foreign investment and the operation of foreign enterprises can be likened to a battering-ram beating down many obstacles to the introduction of a free-market economy that for over forty years the old system has chosen to ignore" (Dobosiewicz 1992: xii). Some advocates predict that foreign direct investment can "rub off" on their culturally inferior domestic competitors: "As a small nucleus in the economies of Eastern Europe, FDI can generate spillover effects far in excess of its own magnitude" (Svetlicic, Artisien, and Rojec 1993: 10). This "demonstration effect"—the transmission of the "modern" culture—is not limited to the economy. Foreign investment, to its more zealous advocates, will create a modern institutional and political environment. For example, "Their superior efficiency, productivity, and profitability create a potent 'demonstration effect' whose influence is increasingly felt in the political sphere as well" (Dobosiewicz 1992: xii). Or, "Foreign investment can also affect positively the transformation process in the region through its impact on government policies and the adoption of liberal regulations regarding banking, accounting, currency convertibility (and the enlargement of its scope), and business services" (Zloch-Christy 1995: 1).

DEPENDENCY AND WORLD SYSTEMS THEORY

Modernization theory's, unabashedly pro-Western and pro-capitalist viewpoint provoked a fierce backlash in the form of dependency and world systems theory. The most famous theorist working from the dependency perspective is Andre Gunther Frank. Frank argues that capitalism is a system that developed in Europe and now encompasses the entire world. The entire world is linked together by a "chain of metropolises and satellites, which runs from the world metropolis down to the hacienda or rural merchant who are satellites of the local commercial metropolitan center but who in their turn have peasants as their satellites" (Frank 1967: 150). Through these chains linking metropolis and satellite economic surplus is extracted: "The expropriation and appropriation of a large or even all of and more than the economic surplus or surplus value of the satellite by its local, regional, national, or international metropolis" occurs (150). Thus, this transfer of surplus is responsible both for the development of the metropolis and the underdevelopment of the satellite: "development and underdevelopment each cause and are caused by each other in the total development of capitalism" (Frank 1967: 150). Indeed, "the more intimate the past contact of these regions with the metropolis, the more underdeveloped they are today" (Frank 1967: 351).

Thus, as a result of the historical development of capitalism, the economies of the underdeveloped countries have been transformed to meet the requirements of the metropolis. These countries were organized for the production and export of raw materials to the metropolis, and in turn import manufactured items from the metropolis. Often, this requires the destruction of local manufacturing and industry. This may occur either directly, by force, or through competition with larger, foreign companies.

The consequences of this transformation on the economy are enormous. First, raw materials have declining terms of trade. Thus, capital flows to the satellite through exchange. Second, dependence generates inequality in the satellite. As a result, the majority have little money to buy locally produced consumer goods, and the elite purchase luxury goods made in the metropolis. Third, because most businesses are foreign-owned, they repatriate profits to the satellite, thereby causing even more surplus drain.

As a result of these mechanisms, Frank concludes that economic development is impossible within capitalism. "National capitalism and national bourgeoisie do not and can not offer any way out of underdevelopment" (Frank 1967: 215). Instead, countries that form the satellites of the world system can only develop if they break from the world capitalist system and initiate autarkic socialist development.

Wallerstein builds on Frank's approach when he theorizes the world system. According to Wallerstein, a stratified world system develops with capitalism. While Frank sees the world system as a series of metropolis-satellite chains, Wallerstein sees one world system which is stratified between the core, semi-periphery and periphery. Different parts of the world have different organizations of production, because each type "is best suited for particular types of goods" (Wallerstein 1974: 91). The end result is a system in which there is a core with free labor, a periphery with coerced cash-crop production, and a semi-periphery with sharecropping.

While Frank's world system is frozen, and no underdeveloped country can develop at all within the framework of capitalism, Wallerstein thinks it is possible that countries may "move up" the world system into the "semi-periphery." Wallerstein describes this process of change in the world system in the following manner: "Indeed, it may well be that in this kind of system it is not structurally possible to avoid, over a long period of historical time, a circulation of elites in the sense that the particular country that is dominant at a given time tends to be replaced in this role sooner or later by another country" (Wallerstein 1974: 350). However, despite these few differences, Wallerstein also identifies a flow of surplus from the periphery to the core as the cause of the impoverishment of the former, and the simultaneous development of the latter. This is accomplished through trade, in which an international division of labor exists, in which "tasks requiring higher levels of skill and greater capitalization" occur in the core, which thereby earns them greater rewards (Wallerstein 1974: 350).

Many other studies from the dependency school identify foreign investment as the main cause of a number of problems that contribute to the growing disparity between the economic performance of the advanced economies and the Third World. Such arguments focus on issues of inequality, the creation of low-wage jobs in the tertiary sector, overurbanization, overpopulation, and slow growth (Chase-Dunn 1975; Evans and Timberlake 1980; Timberlake and Kentor 1983; Bornschier and Chase-Dunn 1985; Bradshaw 1987; London 1987, 1988). Indeed, many authors writing from this perspective argue that the placement of industrial capital in developing countries via foreign direct investment has created a system of "dependent" capitalism or "neo-colonialism" that essentially replaces formal colonialism of the mercantilist era (Galtung 1971; Cardoso and Faletto 1979; Bornschier and Chase-Dunn 1985; Landsburg 1979).

According to the dependency school, the primary mechanism for this deleterious state of affairs is market penetration by foreign capital which crowds out domestic productive capacity and captures the domestic market. Profits from these activities flow back to the core and lead to a lack of local investment and thus economic stagnation. Therefore, while foreign direct investment may spur growth in the short run, in the long run it will lead to poor economic performance.

A number of observers of the Eastern European environment place a negative evaluation on the impact of most foreign investment on the countries involved. The most telling critique is that foreign investment has been essentially market-destroying (see Matzner 1995). Market-destroying behavior primarily consists of buying the distribution networks for domestic output and replacing domestically produced goods with foreign-produced commodities. Perhaps the most famous example of this (although they skipped the "buying" part) is the British destruction and replacement of the indigenous Indian fabric and textile industry (see Baran 1957: 144–150).

In Eastern Europe the Hungarian example of Tungsrum, the giant light bulb maker, provides a well-known case of such predatory behavior. Others have commented on the purchasing of markets for excess production in Hungary:

Those foreign investors who bought existing assets usually conserved the market structure. They were for the most part content with buying a company and acquiring its market share in the Hungarian economy, so they just kept running production or *instead sold their own products through the sales network of the purchased company. Since the Hungarian maker is shared by usually two to five companies, the foreign investor at once acquired 20–30 percent of the market, securing for himself an oligopolistic position whereby the need to modernize equipment or increase the market share was not compelling.* (Bakos 1995: 102) [Emphasis added]

In addition, Bakos believes that

it is pretty obvious that FDIs and JVs have not had a positive quantitative effect on employment while taking over or buying into a Hungarian company; more advanced technologies and higher organizational standards require a smaller labor force. (119)

Furthermore, supposedly, foreign investors use non-Hungarian suppliers, thereby decreasing overall domestic economic demand:

foreign capital appearing in Hungary relies not on Hungarian subsuppliers but on its own home-based subsidiaries and satellites. (119)

Thus we have two radically different ways of thinking about interaction between Western and noncapitalist economies, and more specifically about the effects of foreign investment on developing or transforming economies. Both approaches, in spite of their differences, share a simplified understanding of foreign investment—this chapter seeks to move beyond these Manichean paradigms towards a more balanced approach.

THE REAL IMPACT OF FOREIGN CAPITAL ON THE TRANSITION FROM SOCIALISM IN CENTRAL AND EASTERN EUROPE

The economic success of the West relative to Soviet-style economies, combined with increased travel to and contact with the West by technocrats, strongly contributed to the delegitimization of state socialism for this extremely important segment of the power structure in late-socialist societies. Ironically, just as the economic success of the West hit home psychologically in Eastern Europe, the West itself experienced a serious economic crisis. The economic crisis in the

West, beginning from 1966 to 1973 in the United States and elsewhere, included the massive increase in interest rates that helped created the debt trap in Poland and Hungary. This debt helped undermine the economic performance of these systems—inhibiting the steady growth that was the material basis of the consent granted to the socialist elites by broader stratums of society.

While the ideological impact of foreign capital in causing the collapse of Communism should not be underestimated, its expected dominant role in creating capitalism has not emerged everywhere. Direct foreign investment into Eastern Europe has been much lighter than previously envisioned.

To date, the East European countries, with a combined population of over 400 million, have attracted FDI stocks comparable with those of Ireland, Norway and Austria, each with a population less than five million. Industrial market economies, with an average income per head equal to that of the most prosperous East European economies, have attracted fifty times more investment per head of population. (Svetlicic, Artisien, and Rojec 1993: 9)

While foreign direct investment may not be the most important story in the making of capitalism in Eastern Europe, it is still undoubtedly an important phenomenon—and is becoming more important (see United Nations 1996: 64). Indeed, Hungary accounts for 9934, and the Czech Republic 5008, out of the 33,565 million U.S. dollars worth of FDI in the region up through 1995 (United Nations 1996: 64).

Aggregate measures of foreign direct investment do not tell us much about the actual effects of foreign direct investment—about what type of firms are created by this activity. The Tarki data sets allow us to get a rough breakdown on the types of firms with significant foreign ownership in Hungary. In 1992, 21.6 percent of the top 3000 firms in Hungary were 30 percent or more owned by foreign owners—a very high amount. Nearly one in five firms has major, and most often dominant, foreign ownership.

Contra the expectations of large privatization of huge state firms, the data indicate that foreign firms are smaller than average (see Table 4.1). They are overrepresented among firms with less than 100 employees, while they are quite underrepresented in the larger firms. My fieldwork suggests that these smaller firms are mostly joint ventures with former managers, often employing what I call the "clone company" strategy.

Table 4.1
Comparison of Firm Size to Amount of Foreign Ownership

Employees	*FDI < 30%*	*FDI ≥ 30%*	*Number of Firms*
≤ 100	73.2%	26.8%	526
101 to 300	79.1%	20.9%	234
301 to 1000	91.0%	9.0%	177
1001 to 3000	84.3%	15.7%	51
more than 3000	84.6%	15.4%	13

So, if the firms on average are smaller than other firms without foreign investment, what sectors of the economy are they likely to occupy? Appendix 4 shows the sectoral breakdown of foreign investment. Foreign ownership is disproportionately large among industrial firms and firms engaged in commerce, and underrepresented by a large amount in agriculture, transport, and building. This tells us only that foreign firms are not heavily overrepresented among firms in commerce, as might be expected if one views foreign firms as parasitically involved in the sphere of trade. On the other hand, the overrepresentation in industry is interesting. From a neoclassical perspective, this is to be expected, as these firms should seek to take advantage of East Europe's comparative advantage—cheap skilled labor in close proximity to Western Europe.

Evidence of the importance of joint ventures can be found in Appendix 5, on the origins of companies with 30 percent or more foreign ownership. We see that a significant number of these firms reported prior ownership as being "fully state" or "partly state." Many of these must be manager clone companies or management or employee buy-outs of divisions of state-owned enterprises. Appendix 6 gives us even more information in this regard. We find a significant number of firms listing prior ownership by state companies and coops. Surely, the very large number of firms that listed limited liability companies as their prior form suggests many "clone" companies or management buy-out groups.

Both dependency theorists and modernization theorists would expect foreign ownership to be associated with profitable firms, either because they are parasitic or because they are more efficient and thus outcompete domestically owned firms. Indeed, firms with at least 30 percent foreign ownership are disproportionately profitable, as Table 4.2 attests.

While the statistics are interesting, only my fieldwork offered a hope of beginning to understand the precise nature of foreign investment. Again, what I discovered in my fieldwork was the need to disaggregate foreign investment. Different modalities of foreign investment are created by the alternative strategies pursued by socialist managers, technocrats, and aspiring entrepreneurs (some of whom were former political dissidents). I identified four types of foreign direct investment: (1) small joint-ventures with former managers; (2) large enterprise

Table 4.2
Rate of Profit and Foreign Ownership

Profitability (net profit over assets)	Less than 30% foreign	30% or more foreign	Total firms
No profits	80.1%	19.9%	492
0–10%	80.3%	19.7%	335
10–20%	67.6%	32.4%	68
20–50%	70.8%	29.2%	65
50+%	59.0%	41.0%	41
Total	78.4%	21.6%	1001

privatization by multinational corporations; (3) the establishment of new businesses owned by foreign owners; (4) large joint-ventures.

SMALL JOINT-VENTURES

One strategy of combining with foreign capitalists is to create small joint ventures by employing a strategy I refer to as creating a "clone company" in chapter 2. A manager pursuing this strategy forms a private company that is a duplicate or "clone" of his or her old division (or part of a division) of the state-owned enterprise that formerly employed him or her.

The foreign variety of this process consists of forming a clone company, and then negotiating a business arrangement between the clone company and a representative of a foreign firm. Typically the manager met this representative during the socialist period. The foreign partner may be a part-owner of the firm, thereby establishing a joint venture; or they may have a symbiotic relationship, based on the local firm either selling the products of the foreign firm, or producing commodities for export to the home country of the foreign enterprise. This process creates much smaller firms than one might expect, given popular conceptions of the huge multinational companies that people usually associate with foreign direct investment. They usually employ 50 people or less.

The advantage of this kind of foreign investment is that it provides the postcommunist firm with capital for daily operating expenses and especially for investment, both of which are very scarce in the postcommunist context. For any firms not able to participate in "clientelist" networks with banks, this might be the only way to get significant amounts of investment capital. In addition, the firm gains access both to foreign products and to foreign markets. The economy as a whole benefits, since an increase in market entrants reduces monopolization. Subcontracting arrangements also provide postcommunist firms with an outlet for their very abundant excess capacity. These firms have the additional advantage of creating a structure of ownership and control whereby the Hungarian partner effectively controls the firm: this scenario increases the likelihood of the reinvestment of profits in the local economy.

I came across several examples of this in my fieldwork in Hungary. I will discuss two cases—one in which there was only a commercial relationship formed with foreign capital, the other in which foreign capital became an owner.

The first company, HospitalCo., is 100 percent privately owned by the president and founder of the company. HospitalCo. does sales, service, exhibitions and presentations of high-tech medical equipment imported from Danish, French, British and American firms. The founder was an employee of the Hungarian Academy of Sciences since 1975, and was basically engaged in the same activity then as now. A Danish company with which he had developed a long-term relationship approached him in 1990 with the idea of forming a private company to distribute their product to the Hungarian market.

He founded the company in 1990 with one million HUF and started distributing equipment made by other European firms. The company grew to have total assets in 1995 worth 25 million HUF and employed 15 people. Although the three competitors he had in 1990 have now grown to five, he has been able to keep 60 to 70 percent of the market share.

This firm was much like many other small firms in Hungary. It received no type of state subsidy and was not involved in any complicated interenterprise ownership schemes or networks of firms. It was just a simple market-dependent private enterprise owned and controlled by one person. He financed his day-to-day operations with loans from the National Bank of Hungary, although he complained bitterly about the extremely high interest rates (about 30 percent). He claimed he could not get any loans to expand his business, since, as everyone knew, this required connections and bribes (see my discussion of the clientelistic allocation of finance capital in chapter 2). He also complained about the very high tax rate, as well as its constantly changing nature. The tax environment, ever-present inflation, shrinking demand, and pervasive interenterprise debt has made him extremely pessimistic about the future of his business. He said he now puts most of his money into banks so that he can benefit from the high interest rates.

In this case, the role of foreign capital was benign if limited. It was not replacing any indigenous productive capacity, since these commodities were imported prior to the transition. All the companies, with the exception of the American firm, were willing to give him the stock prior to payment, thereby making possible transactions in an economic environment rife with liquidity problems and pervasive interenterprise debt. He reports regularly consulting with the Dutch firm that was his main supplier for marketing and technical advice—fulfilling the modernization expectation that foreign contact would bring Western technology and know-how to non-Western economies. Furthermore, foreign involvement brought new market entrants, creating a competitive business environment where there was once monopoly. (Although this is not too consequential; the market is extremely small and could not support many more entrants.)

A case of forming a partnership with foreign capital ownership was GateCo. I interviewed the president and half-owner of the company. The other 50 percent is owned by a German company. For 30 years the Hungarian owner worked for a state company that processed metal, starting as a technician. For the last seven years he was the director of the division that planned metal construction. When he made buildings he realized that the gates and doors were of insufficient quality. So he looked for a Western company to make them. In 1986, during a large European trade exhibit, he met his current business partner. This future partner expressed interest in working with the state-owned enterprise, but in 1986 the manager did not have the freedom to make a deal. In 1988 Hungary allowed his division to start importing gates from his future partner. Then in 1990, the law changed to allow the formation of joint-stock companies.

By 1990 the interviewee had become the director of the division of the state-owned enterprise that made and repaired gates. He described his motivation to form his company as stemming from his frustration with the way the state-owned enterprise was run. Things were simply too bureaucratic, and permission from the hierarchy was required for all activities, even for simple practices like fixing gates they had installed. By the time he received permission to fix something, he said, the owner of the gate had either already fixed it, or more likely, something else now needed to be fixed.

Apparently fed up with the situation, the interviewee asked the German gatemaker if they still wanted to form a partnership, which they did. The initial capital was one million forints, with each side contributing half. At first, GateCo. simply imported gates made in Germany and sold them on the Hungarian market. He took about ten workers from his old division with him, but all but two have quit because of the greater demands of work, compared to the old state-owned company. They work 6 AM to 8 PM, with no vacations or holidays for the first three years. But, he pointed out, he demands even more of himself.

In its five years of operation, his company has grown substantially, if not spectacularly. Its assets are now 35 million forints (US $270,000), a large increase from the initial one million. He has gone from 10 employees up to 20, with 16 engaged in production and servicing, and four with administration. His wife heads the staff and keeps the books. Of his 16 nonclerical workers, he always has six located in Germany making gates. They earn very high pay, and, he stressed, "learn how to work hard." He rotates these workers every two years, and he said it has been an effective motivator, as predicted by modernization theory. Also, it helps retain his skilled workers.

While it initially only imported gates from his German partner, GateCo. now imports gates from French and Spanish companies as well. As a result, the company has increased the variety of styles it carries. He explained that one of the advantages of importing gates is that when demand falls, he doesn't have to lay off his employees. Currently, out of the 18 foreign and domestic companies selling automated gates, his company has 20 percent of the market share, worth about 100 million HUF ($770,000) in turnover per year. He has three vans that service these automated gates.

One of the great fears about foreign capital participation is that it will replace domestic productive capacity. Indeed, GateCo. imported and sold gates made abroad. However, GateCo. has started to produce about half the gates it sells, and the company buys its inputs from domestic producers.

This company seems clearly beneficial to the Hungarian economy. As the company grew, it reinvested much of its profits in Hungary. It provided jobs to the Hungarian population and increased aggregate demand by purchasing domestic inputs for the gates it produced locally.

Moreover, it would seem that the modernization school was correct, in that the owner and employees in this company had "Western" or perhaps "entrepreneurial" values. The owner stressed that it was his exposure to "another way of doing things" when he worked and traveled through Western Europe that made him want to run his own company. He emphasized that his company's slogan is "consumer first." He aims for customer satisfaction, and thus is able to retain his customers for a long time. His policy is to repair his product as soon as a call comes in, never waiting for the next business day, no matter how close they are to closing time. Indeed, a secularized version of the "Protestant ethic" was obviously apparent during the interview. The interviewee was dressed very plainly, and the office was functional without any signs of luxury.

This former socialist manager did not appear to take part in any subterranean redistribution or clientelistic relationships. In fact, when I asked about his source of investment capital, he burst out laughing, saying the question proved my ignorance of the Hungarian economic environment. Any small firm that operates with bank loans, he explained, was doomed to failure because of the enormous interest rates. Moreover, he emphatically stated that even qualifying for a bank loan required connections and bribes. Not only did he not receive any subterranean redistribution, he actively avoided the state. He complained bitterly of the high rate of taxation, and explained that whenever possible, he did "black work" that would go unreported to the state. He estimated he did about 10 percent of his work this way. He didn't feel bad about not reporting income at all, because, as he explained, the state doesn't help when he creates jobs, doesn't help him train workers, doesn't stop the oil mafia when they are cheating him, and doesn't stop the "big dogs" when they don't pay taxes on imports.

In stark contrast to this example, there is a more familiar variety of foreign investment: a multinational privatizes a large state-owned enterprise. This too results from a distinct managerial strategy, in which old socialist managers seek to become members of the upper management of a foreign multinational corporation that privatizes their old state-owned enterprise. Managers help multinationals by concealing their firms' assets to reduce the cost of privatization, or at least by providing accurate information about their enterprises. This strategy is sometimes referred to as becoming a member of a *"comprador intelligentsia"* (Szelenyi 1995, Eyal, Szelenyi and Townsley forthcoming), a term which implies that these managers grow wealthy by assisting foreigners in gaining economic control and dominance of their society.

This is an attractive strategy for most managers, as the wealth and prestige that go along with being a member of the management of a foreign multinational are quite substantial. Managers are not disproportionately fired in this situation: 24.5 percent of foreign-owned firms in the 1996 Tarki data set report a change in management planned for 1997, compared to 28.6 percent for state-owned enterprises and 29.3 percent for enterprises with significant state and private ownership, although manager-owned (15.6 percent) and employee-owned firms (14.3 percent) report lower turnover rates. Often, these managers earn extremely high salaries.

The privatized firm is almost always strengthened by the capital, management expertise and market access such privatization brings. The key to selecting this strategy involves having a buyer, a possibility only if the firm has some potential for international marketing or has a large chunk of the Hungarian domestic market.

One such case is the pharmaceutical producer Pharmco. in the Czech Republic. PharmCo. was founded in 1883 by an Austrian industrialist, and was nationalized in 1945. In 1952 it was renamed PharmCo. From 1945 to 1990 it was part of SPOFA, the state holding company for pharmaceuticals. SPOFA was disbanded in 1990, and its constituent companies became independent. In January 1994, PharmCo. became a joint-stock company, and in July 1994 the American multinational IVAX bought 60 percent of its shares.

The firm has a wide range of pharmaceutical activities consisting primarily of liquid pharmaceuticals, in which it was forced to specialize exclusively when under SPOFA's control. Its most important commodity, its "goose that lays the golden egg," according to one interviewee, the Czech President and Chairman of the Board, is its ability to produce Cyclosporin-A, which is used for kidney transplants and child immunity diseases. This was what attracted the interest of foreign capital. PharmCo. is one of two producers in the world able to manufacture this product.

PharmCo. sells the majority of its product on the Czech and Slovak markets, another 15.3 percent to the rest of Eastern Europe, and 26.5 percent to the rest of world. Their comparative advantage is that they have some very good chemical processes and the Cyclosporin-A, and they are very skilled in liquid pharmaceuticals. They have highly skilled and specialized labor coupled with very low wages, although these have been going up. Being forced to specialize in liquids, their weakness resides in having an essentially obsolete product portfolio.

Their strategy is to expand and rebuild their market in the Eastern Block. Because of very high levels of protectionism, they are not too ambitious to expand into the Western markets. In addition, the United States has very strict patent laws, and it is quite difficult to obtain a noninfringing formulation of consupren (the final form of Cyclosporin-A).

To overcome these challenges, PharmCo. decided to collaborate with a foreign partner. They ran a "controlled auction" in order to generate competition and obtain the best bid. The process began in 1992 and took far longer than anticipated. Finally, in 1995, PharmCo. became majority-owned by an American multinational which bought 62 percent of all shares. This company, IVAX, is a rapidly growing integrated health care company with an annual turnover of 1.3 billion USD. It is the largest generic drug producer in the world and employs about 8000 people. It is a vertically integrated company, and PharmCo. now adds one more division to the corporation.

It seems that purchasing 62 percent of shares completely guaranteed IVAX's control of PharmCo. The interviewee said that whoever owned the other 38 percent was of no consequence. This is borne out by the membership of the Supervisory Board and the Board of Directors. Five of seven members from the Board of Directors are from IVAX, and the other two are from PharmCo.'s old management. Of the nine members of the Supervisory Board, the Chairman and five other members are from IVAX, one is from another American corporation, and two are former managers from PharmCo.

I spoke with the newly appointed Chief Operating Officer, a British man hired by IVAX to oversee operations. He functions like a second chief executive officer, with whom the old CEO and President would now have to work, and, in essence, report to. According to these two interviewees, PharmCo. was going to be significantly streamlined and restructured. The marketing and sales departments would be massively expanded (doubled or tripled in size), and management planned to reduce the workforce from 1300 to between 900 and 950. The long-range strategy was to turn PharmCo. into a high-quality generic-drug producer selling primarily in Eastern Europe. The decision to focus on generic drugs was necessitated by the enormous cost of launching a new product in the pharmaceutical industry. The research and development costs of the typical product are one billion dollars, not to mention the heavy advertising costs associated with the pharmaceutical industry.

Again, we see that foreign-owned firms have strong ownership, tight control, and a clear business strategy. This firm had no interenterprise ownership and did not receive any type of subterranean redistribution. Foreign ownership, then, seemed to bring many of the benefits promised by modernization theory. This included badly needed foreign capital to modernize PharmCo.'s outdated production capabilities. Although they also borrow from foreign and domestic banks, their modernization was to be primarily financed by IVAX. Securing the much lower interest rates of foreign loans would seem unlikely without IVAX's ownership; foreign banks are not interested in loaning to Eastern European companies which do not plan to sell on the Western market, since currency instability could make repayment very difficult.

In this case, the *comprador intelligentsia* had a much more positive effect than their Chinese namesakes who, in the mid-19th century, helped saturate the Chinese market with British-supplied opium. As part of the agreement reached between IVAX and the National Property Fund, PharmCo. will get the right to market all of IVAX's brands on the domestic market, instantly modernizing their portfolio. Heretofore, the Czech Republic had suffered from a severely constricted diversity of drugs, due to the approach formerly taken by the ministry of health, which "planned" the drug industry in the Czech Republic. Thus, the new availability of drugs in the Czech Republic must be seen as a major developmental benefit.

Another example of foreign direct investment by large-scale privatization that I explored was ChocolateCo. in Slovakia. The history of this firm represents, in world system theory's terms, the movement of Slovakia from the capitalist semi-periphery in the late 19th century to the capitalist semi-periphery in the late 20th century.

ChocolateCo. began receiving foreign direct investment in 1896. In 1890 the government in Budapest created numerous incentives in an attempt to spur foreign investment in Greater Hungary. These incentives included a 15-year tax holiday, tax refunds on sugar and cocoa, duty-free imports of machinery and equipment and additional tax relief for the import of raw materials. A German confectionery company, seeking to expand into southeastern Europe, decided to establish a factory in Bratislava—not only to capture the previously mentioned tax breaks, but also to take advantage of the low wages in this part of the Austro-Hungarian empire.

In 1907, establishing itself as a joint-stock company with subsidiaries in Vienna and Budapest, the branch in Bratislava broke away from the German parent company. The company grew quickly, producing primarily marzipan, toffee and peppermint candies. From employing 1000 employees in 1909, it grew to employ 2000 employees prior to the outbreak of World War II (although the blockade in Germany subsequently reduced output and employment significantly).

After the collapse of the Austro-Hungarian empire at the end of World War I, ChocolateCo. attracted Czech investors and adopted a Czech name in addition to its Hungarian and German names. In 1931 its name was "Slovakized" (by adding *-ovia* to its end) and it registered with the Czechoslovak commercial registry. The Great Depression and the crash of the New York Stock Exchange hit the company very hard, requiring the layoff of many workers. The company finally recovered just in time for World War II.

Not physically damaged by the war, the company actually expanded its product line and production capacity during this time, only to be seized by the Red Army in April of 1945. It then provided the Red Army with confectionery and artificial honey until it was handed over to three "national administrators" appointed by the Czechoslovak state in July of 1945. German and Hungarian staff members were expelled from the company and, on September 10, 1946, the company's assets were seized because of its German origin. By this time, the company had only 200 employees.

In January 1947, the company was formally nationalized and its assets were transferred to a new national company called the Slovak Factories for Chocolate, Confectionery and Fruit Products with headquarters in Bratislava. In 1948 the authorities decided to have the plant specialize only in confectionery, and in 1953 the company was incorporated into the new Slovak Bakeries enterprise. The company would undergo several more organizational changes, being moved from one socialist conglomerate to the other, falling under the jurisdiction of one ministry or the other. The last change occurred in 1988, when ChocolateCo. became part of Confectionery s.p., also a state-owned company. By the end of these changes ChocolateCo. held about 36 percent of the domestic market in cocoa, 20 percent in chocolate bars, and 18 percent in chocolate confectionery.

In 1992 the National Property Fund, the sole shareholder, established ChocolateCo. as a joint-stock company. By direct sale, 67 percent of the stock was purchased by the largest European coffee and confectionery producer, Jacob Suchard, for 600 million SK. Thus, almost 100 years after it was founded, the company returned to German ownership. This was not to last long, however, as Jacob Suchard was then acquired by Kraft which, in turn, is owned by Philip Morris Companies, Inc., the biggest producer of packaged foods worldwide.

This privatization closely mirrors the managerial strategy elaborated above. Part of the privatization agreement was that no managers would be fired during the first several years. The supervisory board, with the exception of the director from Kraft headquarters, was composed entirely of local managers. The Board of Directors consisted of all local management as well. In addition, ChocolateCo. conducts salary surveys three to four times a year and ensures above-average compensation for their management. For example, the average wage for Slovak managers is 7470 SK per month, while ChocolateCo. managers average 9000 SK a month.

Being part of a multinational corporation has the advantage of providing a source of investment capital which doesn't burden the company with enormous debts. The look of the factory and office was far different from the domestically owned businesses I visited. Compared to the decaying buildings and shabby interior of some of the domestic firms, ChocolateCo. looked ultramodern. Indeed, to even enter the office complex I went through a security check complete with bag searches and a metal detector. (And this was for nothing more than a chocolate factory. The element of secrecy combined with the overpowering smell of chocolate in the air made me feel like I was doing an interview at Willy Wonka's Chocolate Factory.)

Thus, unlike in many companies privatized by local investments, foreign investment in ChocolateCo. resulted in strong ownership able to set a coherent strategy and provide capital for investment. The first reorganization to occur after privatization was the creation of a sales and marketing department. Then, ChocolateCo. launched a massive modernization program. Since 1992, Philip Morris has invested 400 million SK ($13.3 million) in the company to bring it up to Western European production standards. Thus the company has invested in only three years almost as much as it paid for the company. The result is that after only three years of operation, the company has gained 40 percent of the chocolate market in Slovakia, its main competitor being another multinational, Nestle, which privatized a chocolate factory in Prague. Last year, ChocolateCo. launched ten new products. They have begun to export as well, mainly to Russia and the Ukraine, which now accounts for one-third of their turnover.

While it is true, at least theoretically, that local ownership would perhaps reinvest more of the profits in the region, this may well be compensated for by higher productivity, the resulting higher growth, and finally the higher absolute levels of reinvestment. It seems unlikely that keeping the company in local hands would have been a superior option from a developmental perspective. With the exception of the managers of MegaChem and the creators of Czech Business Groups, which included banks and firms engaging in political capitalism, the managers of all other domestically owned firms complained about the complete lack of capital for investment.

This case of privatization by a foreign multinational brought all those things neoclassical economists and modernization theorists expected: investment capital, Western technology and know-how, a strong private owner and a clear business strategy. There were no complex interenterprise ownership strategies such as I found with domestic companies. ChocolateCo. owned only one other company—

a Prague-based subsidiary which distributed their product in the Czech Republic. They did not simply buy the Slovak market, but continued to produce with local people. Indeed, by paying higher-than-average wages they increased the aggregate demand in Slovakia.

One advantage of foreign direct investment over indigenous ownership is that the latter often requires local financing (see chapter 5) because management buy-outs usually necessitate a great deal of borrowing. Without this debt burden, the foreign-owned firm can produce for export with a lower per-unit cost and thereby increase its world market share.

This type of foreign direct investment can, however, be abused. Large privatizations can be market destroying. For Hungarian supermarkets this is clearly the case. Bought by German multinationals, Hungarian food retail stores carry mostly German and European foodstuffs. Hungarian agriculture, once the showpiece of "Goulash Socialism," has experienced a devastating crisis that literally cut the output of this sector in half. Another example involves the Hungarian plant oil market, of which several firms were purchased via privatization by a Dutch company, thereby creating a foreign monopoly as the sole distributor. Prices subsequently doubled.

In addition to privatization, subsidiaries of multinational firms have expanded dramatically and are now significant economic actors. One example is HP Czech Republic. I conducted an interview with the District Sales Manager—one of the Czech founders of HP Czech Republic. He has been with the company for 16 years and was responsible for the Czechoslovakia area in terms of computers and medical products sales for the last six years. HP Czech Republic, then, was operating in some form well into the Communist period.

In 1968, HP Geneva decided to sell personal computers in Czechoslovakia. Not having an office there, a representative performed technical consultation and made sales of computers and medical technology through HP Vienna. They had no official presence, and sales were never over five million USD. They established an office in 1979 which existed until 1991. (The interviewee referred to this jokingly as the enlightenment period—which is perfectly congruent with modernization theory.) This organization was still part of the Vienna office, making sales but giving no support, employing two people at the beginning of the period and ending with twelve employees in 1991. Their maximum turnover was 12 million USD. Computer support was provided by two subcontracting companies—one in the Czech Republic and one in Slovakia.

In 1991, HP Czech Republic established a wholly owned subsidiary similar to the ones HP established in Poland and Hungary. From 12 employees the subsidiary rapidly grew to 150 to 160 people. In fact, their greatest obstacle to further growth has been the difficulty of hiring additional staff; they currently have ten to fifteen vacancies. Turnover grew by more than 50 percent in 1995 to 130 million dollars.

HP Czech Republic sells a range of computer-related items as well as "systems" products. The actual manufacturing takes place not in the Czech Republic, but in the high-wage countries (Germany, France, Spain and the UK). Their customers are not individuals but rather corporations in manufacturing industries, as well as government and parastatal agencies.

The interviewee said that much of their success stems from the fact that Czech companies want to deal with a foreign company when they wish to purchase a high-tech item like a computer. In addition, the company had also developed significant goodwill as a result of their (relatively) long history of doing business in the Czech Republic. According to the interviewee, HP even took losses to provide service parts. Ten years later, he points out, this policy is now paying off, as HP wins contracts over newer market entrants.

While HP certainly does not gain any advantage from subterranean redistribution, they have conducted much business with the Czech state. After the collapse of the Communist regime, the government received money from the European Union to modernize. Most of this money ended up in HP's coffers. In 1991 the Czech government gave a contract to HP for more than ten million US dollars (out of a total turnover of twelve million). They also have been awarded the contracts for two of the three new logistics and financial projects undertaken by the Czech military. The Czech Power company, the largest economic organization in the Czech Republic, is another big customer. In the financial markets they supply insurance companies, investment funds and banks (including the Czech National Bank and the Commercial Bank). Most recently, they were awarded a contract with Czech Telecom.

The interviewee explained that the primary difference between the way the business is presently conducted and the way it was conducted during the Communist period resulted from the elimination of the involvement of state trading monopolies. Previously, KOVO, a foreign trade organization, had always sold to the final customer. The elimination of the Communist intermediary was not a positive development, because whereas KOVO always paid, HP can no longer be assured they will receive payment from a customer. As a result they have had to establish a credit department and frequently request payment in advance.

Like the other foreign-owned firms in my study, HP Czech Republic does not participate in a complicated web of interfirm relations and does not exhibit any qualities of recombinant property. They cooperate with other companies to provide programs for their hardware in writing, just as HP does in every country. Quite simply, they exemplify a multinational, capitalist enterprise that is dominating a local market as a result of their reputation and a quality product.

Their relationship with both the government and various banks are of a "friendly but formal" character. The interviewee stated that the government gives them no interference. In fact, they even ask HP for an opinion when formulating laws. He also pointed out that they enjoy very positive relationships with various banks. This friendliness with banks does not stem from any financial arrangements, as HP only occasionally takes short-term loans from local banks.

HP Czech Republic, while not contributing to a scarcity of local capital for investment, does provide employment. Like all foreign ownership in my study, HP almost exclusively employs local manpower. Out of 150 employees, only three are expatriates. HP has adopted this policy, according to the interviewee, because Czechs believe that a Czech-speaking American passport holder, earning Western European or American pay (around 30 times the local pay), is not an acceptable coworker.

Aside from employment, one can ask if HP is taking markets away from domestic producers. The answer is clearly no. HP's competitors are Digital and IBM—the Czech Republic has never had the capacity to produce high-quality computer hardware. Even if they were to begin, one would question the use of government and military items that fall below the very best available technological standards.

FOREIGN CAPITAL AND POLITICAL DISSIDENTS

Another path that foreign direct investment takes occurs through the formation of an alliance with domestic holders of political capital. An example from my field-work was TV Nova, one of two private Czech TV stations. Competing in a field of five stations, this company enjoys enormous success, and has expanded dramatically since it was founded in 1993. The Kagen Group, a TV rating/analysis group, called TV Nova the most successful TV station in Europe and perhaps the world. No other station operating in a situation of both public and private TV is as successful. This is reflected in the company's economic results. Whereas a TV station usually takes five to seven years to show a profit, Nova was profitable after only nine months.

Its stock, issued on NASDAQ in mid-1994, became the most successful initial public offering in the United States that year. It started at 14,4 per share and is now at 23 to 25 points per share. With 400 employees, they have captured about 70 percent of the viewing market for most time slots and had a turnover of about 3 billion crowns last year. Their closest rival is the state-owned Czech TV 1, which employs 4000, has state subsidies equal to the entire Czech TV advertising budget of 2.1 billion crowns and is allowed to use advertising as well. Despite this arrangement, which significantly reduces the price of advertising (thus disproportionately hurting the non-subsidized Nova), Nova still massively outcompetes them on the market.

The ownership and control of Nova is fairly straightforward. The company is really composed of two companies. The first, CET21, is a local Czech Group that received the broadcast license from the state. This group consists of six individual Czech citizens, all former anticommunist dissidents, with the most prominent, my interviewee, being the president of the company. CET21 leases this license to Nova since, by law, foreigners cannot own broadcasting licenses. The ownership of shares is detailed in Table 4.3.

Table 4.3
The Ownership Structure of TV Nova

Owner	Percentage of Shares
Central European Entertainment Group	66%
Czech Savings Bank	22%
CET21	12%

The Central European Entertainment Group is an American-owned, Bermuda-registered,[3] Dutch-based[4] company of which 48 percent is owned by Ronald Lauder, the owner of the multinational cosmetics and clothes company Estée Lauder. The Central European Entertainment Group controls the company firmly with their majority. The Czech Savings Bank is their major creditor, and has been, according to the interviewee, a "good partner" even though they charge very high rates of interest (12 to 13 percent). Not surprisingly, given the bank's ownership stake, this "high" rate is several points lower than most of the other Czech firms in my sample.

The company actually originated as a result of the activity of the present director. He had worked for Czech TV since 1963. During the invasion of 1968 he engaged in clandestine TV coverage and was subsequently blacklisted from all TV stations. He then became a full-time dissident, part of a conservative group of samizdat writers rallying against reform communism. To support himself, he worked under pen names as a script writer. Immediately after the revolution he headed the election campaign of the Civic Forum. After their victory he was appointed as a senior advisor for the Prime Minister and the official spokesperson for the coalition government. Following the split in the forum (what he designated the defeat of the coalition) he left politics.

Next, he initiated the project for the privatization of an open TV station. This station began to broadcast after the split of the country when the federal channel became available. He founded the CME group and put in a privatization bid over 24 other tenders, including those that had partners with Western media giants such as Murdoch and Turner. His group won despite the fact that Estée Lauder had no experience with broadcasting.

The interviewee was an ardent advocate of "anti-politics" throughout the entire interview (See Eyal 1997). When asked about lobbying, he stressed that Nova donates no money to political groups, even though legislation affecting the company is determined in the parliament. He said lobbying was immoral and seemed fairly shocked by the question.

The secret of Nova's success, he believes, was the company's refusal to become political despite enormous pressure pushing them in this direction, as the prevailing idea advocates a political party having its own media. He pointed out that "Priemera, the other private TV station, is involved in political circles and doing very poorly. Radio Echo was the same way, and has already gone bankrupt. The Telegraph newspaper is also very close to bankruptcy."

Judging by the fare served up by Nova, there seems to be no overt political bias. They show what people want to watch: Czech-dubbed versions of *Dallas*, *MASH*, and Italian- and American-produced soft porn at night. Czechs, like Americans, love this stuff. The interviewee pointed out that TV stations fail because intellectuals who make media want to create a TV station for intellectuals, something they would enjoy themselves. But most viewers are not intellectuals and to be economically successful you have to give viewers what they want.

Nova found its 400 staff members without poaching the talent of the main Czech TV stations. The interviewee said he didn't want to "contaminate" the company with the "diseases" inherited from the state-run firm (which he stated were inefficiency and megalomania). Thus, two-thirds of the employees had never worked for TV before. Some came from different media such as radio, and many were young people with no experience in the field. He pointed out that his company used very tough screening processes to weed out former secret police (unlike the other private station, he informed me, "which is crawling with old secret police").

While Nova owned no firms, they did cooperate with firms to license merchandising and to print a TV guide. They maintained a very clear structure of control. Having no trade unions, Nova made individual agreements with employees.

This firm trajectory certainly doesn't fit Staniszkis' political capitalism thesis, and Stark's theory of "recombinant property" would be hard pressed to be molded to this case (unless it can be argued that the 22 percent owned by a bank which is 30 to 40 percent owned by the government somehow proves it is recombinant property, "neither capitalist nor socialist"). Nee's theory might be plausible, as the manager was very entrepreneurial and did have experience in the second economy of illegal media. However, the creation of this firm was an eminently political process, as the interviewee himself admitted. The fact that he was a prominent dissident with impeccable anticommunist credentials, had been spokesperson for the government and a close advisor of Klaus, and gave such an impassioned plea for anti-politics belied this explanation.

The creation of this firm fits nicely into Szelenyi's theory of the power structure of postcommunism. According to Szelenyi and his collaborators, technocrats joined forces with elements from the "mediacracy and the politocracy" (see Szelenyi, Fodor and Hanley 1996; Eyal, Szelenyi and Townsley, 1998). It seems likely that the selection of his bid over the bids of international media giants, a decision made by a commission reporting to parliament, was not unrelated to his possession of political capital. At the same time, we see a firm emerging which appears to be quite capitalist in every respect. TV Nova, an example of foreign capital joined with local actors, is an unexceptional property form. It has the advantages of Western capital, along with local expertise that emanates from their possession of intimate knowledge of the Czech environment. Of course, the question with foreign ownership is always how much of the profits are to be repatriated. In this instance, it is a fair bet that having two-thirds of shares owned by foreigners means that two-thirds of the dividends will leave the country, at least in the long run.

SUBCONTRACTING

Some privatization by foreign direct investment is not transformative in any way and strongly relies on the subcontracting of products to be sold to Western firms. In this scenario, foreign firms utilize the huge capacity of former socialist firms in order to capture the low cost of labor. Cheap labor, combined with proximity to Western Europe, seems to be the motivating force behind foreign investment in Central European manufacturing that is ultimately intended for export to the West. For example, the average male worker in Western Germany earned $33.21 per hour in 1993, compared to $2.36 per hour in Poland and just $1.76 per hour in the Czech Republic (Knight 1994: 48). One example of this was ClothesCo., which is located on the western border of Hungary.

This firm was founded in 1951 and made light rain jackets sold only in Hungary. In the early 1960s they started selling to the Soviet Union, in the mid-60s to Holland, and then to France and England. By the end of the 1980s they no longer sold to the Eastern block, but exported mostly to the West. Because they were able to sell successfully to Western markets, the regime gave them a great deal of money for technological investment, and, by the mid-1970s, their level of productivity was only slightly below the West European average.

In 1990 they underwent a process of "self-privatization"—a special type of privatization in which a foreign consulting firm approved by the State Property Agency, instead of the State Property Agency itself, does the asset valuation. The resulting ownership structure was 30.6 percent by a consortium of foreign investors, 3.2 percent by domestic Hungarian investors, and the rest by the State Property Agency. In 1995, the foreign owners had increased their share to 50.4 percent, managers and workers received 3 percent, the local government received 5 percent, and the State Property Fund held the rest.

The consortium of foreign owners consists of seven clothing companies (three Austrian, two Italian, one Swedish, and one American) and a British financial service company. The firm's activities consist primarily of using foreign inputs and foreign designs, and using their large (1600 blue-collar workers) and very inexpensive female labor force to stitch the clothes together. The interviewees (the president and chief financial officer) said that no real change in either production or marketing has occurred since the late Communist period. The foreign investors, interested only in their cheap labor, do not invest any funds to raise labor productivity. Indeed, the interviewees stressed that without receiving a major infusion of capital they could not modernize beyond the level they attained in the late 1970s. Even their rate of profit, 6 to 8 percent of gross receipts, has remained constant since the Communist period.

The physical appearance of this company could not be farther from the appearance of ChocolateCo., which was virtually an ideal type of the modern multinational corporation. The building was quite old, the lights in the hallways had all burned out, there was no trace of a high-tech security system to be found, and indeed no high technology to be protected. This was not a company heading towards a high-tech future. Since the transition there has been an increase in competition, but it comes from the other low-wage areas—Poland, the Czech Republic, Romania, the former USSR, and now Brazil (which has the advantage of being closer to the North American market).

THE STRUGGLE BETWEEN FOREIGN AND DOMESTIC CAPITAL

As stated in the second chapter, the structure of the postcommunist economy will partly be shaped by the struggle between actors pushing the agendas of agents based in different types of property. One main locus of struggle will occur between multinational capital and domestic owners. A concrete example of this was MegaChem's public struggle with the International Oil Consortium (a group composed of seven giant Western oil companies) to gain rights to privatize the Czech refinery industry. MegaChem lost as the result of an intensive public relations campaign that painted MegaChem as somehow too "Communist"—too affiliated with the past and Russia. It remains to be seen if the International Oil Consortium will decommission the refineries they bought because they are equipped for Russian oil, rather than the lighter Western crudes they themselves sell.

Another example of this struggle involves the privatization story of LampCo., a firm based in Budapest. This company was originally founded in 1883 in the very same building in which I conducted my interview. It began by making street lamps and, in the 1930s, started to make chemical machinery, which it did for Germany during World War II. Nationalized after the war, the company from that time on exclusively produced chemical machinery.

In 1959 it was amalgamated into a large industrial firm which was also called LampCo. and consisted of six factories, each specializing in a different kind of chemical machinery. This conglomerate was broken up in 1980. Two of the six companies, LampCo. (keeping its original name) and BudaCo., located in Budapest, stayed together. In 1992 BudaCo. became independent and was privatized. In January of 1993 LampCo. was turned into a joint-stock company in order to facilitate privatization, which eventually took place in June of 1995.

This company was privatized by six Hungarians—three were long-time managers from LampCo., and three were managers from other firms in the chemical industry. Together they own 90 percent of the shares. The remaining 10 percent still remain with the State Property Agency, which wants to sell them to the employees, even though the employees only want to purchase 3 percent.

The story of the privatization struggle is a complicated one. Initially, the interviewee, who is one of the six owners, and the managing director, along with one of the directors of a daughter company of one of the six original LampCo companies, formed a limited liability company, LampInvest, that wanted to buy LampCo. At the same time, an association of employees was formed that wanted to purchase 51 percent of the shares and sell 49 percent to the manager-owned limited liability company. The interviewee said this plan was insane, since neither he nor his fellow manager would have reason to invest money in a company unless they could obtain some control of the firm. The manager's company countered with an offer to sell the employee association 35 percent of the shares, which the association promptly rejected (apparently this wasn't insane).

The picture became even more complicated when a French firm that produced the same product entered the privatization picture. At this time LampCo. controlled 93 percent of the domestic market share, with the French company being its only competitor. According to the interviewee, the French firm was facing declining demand at home and hoped to gain LampCo.'s market in Hungary and the former COMECON economies, worth about five million U.S. dollars a year.

The French company's privatization plan was to physically bring their machinery into the plant and then to invest a certain amount in the company. They did not plan on paying the State Property Agency any cash. According to the interviewee, the French company solicited the help of a firm whose director is now the finance minister to lobby the State Property Agency. As a result, he said, LampInvest's first bid to privatize the company in 1993 was rejected because of a minor technicality. Resubmitting the bid in August of 1994, they found themselves competing against the French company, which won the bid. However, the French company refused to sign the agreement, hoping to force a lowering of the price. As LampInvest still had their bid submitted, the State Property Agency reluctantly accepted it. When the French company put in another bid six weeks later for 2 percent more money, the State Property Agency canceled their agreement with LampInvest. LampInvest took the State Property Agency to court, won the right to privatize the company, and was awarded 7 million HUF to cover the cost of the trial. The State Property Agency finally signed the privatization agreement in exchange for LampInvest taking only 2.1 million HUF of the 7 million HUF fine.

Thus foreign capital, in all its different modalities, has had an important, although not dominant, role in the transition to capitalism in Eastern Europe. The implications and likely effects of this foreign investment will be discussed in chapter 6, where some quantitative evidence will be mustered on this point.

NOTES

1. Of course, Smith, Marx and Weber wrote on this topic. Marx can be viewed as a modernization theorist because of his view that the capitalist mode of production would

transform all earlier modes of production, as he argued would happen in India. However, after studying Ireland, Marx recognized that capitalist penetration might not so unambiguously lead to development.

2. Modernization theory has been making a comeback of late (see Apter 1990; Chirot 1995).

3. Many U.S. companies locate in Bermuda to avoid taxes.

5

The Managerialization of the Eastern European Economy: Managers and the Transformation of Property

As was argued in the first chapter, while prior transitions to capitalism all occurred in societies with largely precapitalist social structures, one can say that the unique feature of the postcommunist transition to capitalism is that it is occurring in a society with a postcapitalist social structure. One key group of social actors in this postcapitalist landscape consists of firm managers, obvious candidates for the position of a "new class" of the postcommunist social structure. Managers possessed a variety of property rights in reform socialism. They are the group most knowledgeable of the existing productive capacity—the socialist property that the postcommunist governments have or intend to privatize.

One way to restructure all this old property involves finding foreign ownership for firms, as discussed in the last chapter. This is what Szelenyi (1995) calls the path of the *comprador intelligentsia*. Another seemingly logical solution transfers ownership to employees and managers—who better to become the new owners? This has the obvious political appeal of serving justice, inasmuch as the people who worked for years in a company are the people who become owners.[1]

Sociologically, however, management and employee buy-outs have been described as the basis for a political bargain between the technocracy in state economic agencies and banks and elected politicians, managers, and employees. This description has been applied to the former USSR and might well hold in the Eastern European context as well:

Indeed, the collapse of the USSR as the state owner of assets has shifted responsibility for the administration of state-owned enterprises to managers and employees. Moreover, the governments of the newly independent states urgently need to secure the support of workers' unions who have often built up powerful positions within enterprises. The development of management and employee buy-outs may be one means of forming a key coalition of interests between bureaucrats, worker's collectives, managers and political leaders. (Filatotchev, Buck and Wright 1992: 11; as quoted in Ellerman 1993: 3)

Furthermore, an obvious appeal exists in terms of practicality and economic rationality—who else knows better the firm's internal affairs and environment? Who else would know the most efficient way to split up and reconfigure former state assets? As one Eastern European economist argues, "Employees are, by virtue of their position, most knowledgeable about the internal slack, market and technological constraints and opportunities facing the firm" (Bogetic 1993: 468).

THE ECONOMIC APPROACH TO MANAGERIAL AND EMPLOYEE BUY-OUTS

The economic literature on management and employee buy-outs holds certain insights. These insights, however, need to be complemented by a sociological understanding of this phenomenon that directly theorizes issues of power. The research must look beyond the study of formal property rights alone and search out the nonofficial processes and practices that economic sociologists believe often control a large portion of economic activity.

One economic line of argument is that management and employee buy-outs have the "correct" property structure because they provide firm insiders with relatively concentrated ownership, thereby giving them every opportunity and every incentive to exert their maximum effort as efficiently as possible (i.e., "x-efficiency"). Employee and management ownership internalizes agent-principal externalities—such as the creation of satellite firms as discussed in chapter 2 (see Ellerman 1993: 19). Basically, because the principal and the agent are the same actors, one would expect no shirking or parasitic behavior. These efficiency arguments are even more valid for firms in which management and employees are the biggest owners but there is a free market in shares and a significant number of outside owners. In this situation, the outside owners can keep insiders from prioritizing employment over efficiency and preserving routine ways of doing things (the so-called "immobility of capital" which is the economic argument against worker ownership) (see Bogetic 1993).

Even if the advantages of internalizing "agent-principal externalities" outweigh the disadvantages of the "immobility of capital," there is still a problem with internal buy-outs. In spite of getting subsidized loans, such buy-outs require a high degree of external financing. One source of data in this regard comes from Karsai and Write's 17 case studies of management and employee buyouts (that is, both management and employees bought the firms, which is distinguishable from purely employee buy-outs, in which management has no share ownership). This research showed that in Hungary most firms used extensive credit, as detailed in Table 5.1.

Table 5.1
The Use of Finance in Employee Buy-outs

Number of firms	Percent of privatization sale price paid with credit
2	0%
1	46%
2	50%
1	66%
1	72%
4	75%
5	98%
Total: 16	Average: 63%

Source: Karsai and Write 1994: 1002.

Thus employee buy-outs, according to Karsai and Write, even though made with relatively "cheap" loans by Eastern European standards, result in a very heavy debt burden for the new firms. This deprives the firms of resources needed for restructuring.

This view of "management and employee buy-outs" is informed by a theory developed in advanced capitalist environments—and does not totally account for the transfer of property to firm insiders with all of its relevant dimensions in the postcommunist environment. Postcommunism, like the Communist period itself, has relatively murky property relations, although they are getting clearer as new owners consolidate their control (see Casal's classic statement on property rights under Communism [1980]; and for postcommunism see Szelenyi 1995; Eyal, Szelenyi, and Townsley forthcoming; Stark 1996; Nee 1992a; Oi 1992; Walder 1992a, 1992b). As one top manager of a large chemical firm in Hungary (with mixed private and state ownership) said, "if the waters are too clear, muddy them." In the postcommunist environment property-rights have certainly been "muddy," and indeed somewhat more "malleable" than in "nontransition" economies. In light of this situation, an understanding of how power relations are shaping the emerging new property and market structures in Eastern Europe becomes essential.

A SOCIOLOGICAL UNDERSTANDING OF THE ROLE OF MANAGEMENT AND EMPLOYEE BUY-OUTS: THE MANAGERIALIZATION OF THE POSTCOMMUNIST ECONOMY

Neoclassical discussions of property rights operate with the assumption of *homo economicus* (see Roy 1997). That is, property rights are important insofar as they protect the *natural* inalienability of property (in which a person has a right over an object) against *intrusion* by the state. Thus, property is not conceptualized in a sociological way, which differs by defining it as a social relationship (a person has rights in relation to other persons over the use of an object) which is ultimately guaranteed, and is thus essentially *constituted* by the state.

Indeed, a sociological conception of property rights is crucial to understanding economic activity and economic dynamics, certainly during "transitions" when it is highly doubtful that perfectly regulating markets can be introduced overnight.[2] To be useful, a conception of property rights must move beyond a legalistic framework that focuses exclusively on the legal demarcation of rights—this, by itself, is inadequate even for the "legal-rational" systems of Western Europe and America (see Berle and Means [1932] for the classic statement on this point). Property rights analysis, as a minimum starting point, subdivides property rights into three types: (a) the right to residual income (surplus/profit); (b) the right to control the production process; and (c) the right to transfer property to another (the sale of assets) (Furubotn and Perjovich 1974: 3; Demsetz 1967).

These three types of property rights are logically a subset of social property relations as defined by Brenner: "the relationship among the direct producers, among the class of exploiters (if any exists) [i.e. "owners"], and between the exploiters and producers, which specify and determine the regular and systematic access of individual economic actors (or families) to the means of production and the economic product" (1986: 26).

This notion of property rights adds to the previously mentioned schema by emphasizing both the structured flow of surplus and the relationship between owners as crucial elements of property rights. In a capitalist economy, this relationship between owners includes the market transactions between private firms as well as other linkages (e.g., participation in business groups, joint production, interlocking directorates, cross-ownership). In Konrad and Szelenyi's analysis of socialism (1979), this "inter-exploiter relationship" takes at least two forms. First, there is the relationship between an enterprise and the state (taxation, subsidies and thus budget constraints), which, according to Kornai (1980), is the ultimate cause of economic shortage. Another crucial relationship considers the firm's horizontal relationship with other firms (in Kornai's terminology "vegetative control" [1980]). We will see that these "social property rights" under late socialism provide important resources (by way of residual and informal personal networks) for actors seeking to transform property in the postcommunist period, especially former socialist managers.

THE MANAGERIALIZATION OF THE POSTCOMMUNIST ECONOMY

This chapter seeks to give as detailed an account as possible of the ways in which managers acquire wealth and gain property rights. The sociological account of the position of managers both before and after the transition to capitalism in Eastern Europe places managers somewhere between functioning as junior members of the new power elite and standing squarely in the center of the power structure. According to Szalai, during the period of reform in Hungary, power resided in the hands of the "state and party bureaucracy and the corporate managers" (Szalai 1994: 121). In postcommunism, a "power block" composed of technocrats, managers and dissident intellectuals has emerged (Szelenyi 1995; Eyal and Szelenyi 1997; Eyal, Szelenyi, and Townsley 1998).

Managers, even in the classical period, however, possessed significant property rights. In Hungary, for example, Mihalyi (1992) explains that the state did not really gain all the property rights of firms with nationalization. Enterprise managers obtained all sorts of rights, from the control of daily operations, to decisions over personnel and investments (1992: 5). Managers even had some rights to disposal. "[A]lthough state enterprises were almost never liquidated or sold, they were frequently reorganized, almost always with the input of the managers" (1992: 5). Indeed, the centralization of control in the classical period of socialism actually brought power to the lower rungs of the economic hierarchy (such as enterprise managers), because they were "monopolists" for some products. Thus they could always argue "under such conditions we cannot deliver" (1992: 5), thereby vastly increasing their bargaining power.

The property rights of managers were implicit in the system of "plan bargaining" that emerged in every socialist system. All economic reforms, in Hungary as well as elsewhere, generally served to increase the power of the enterprise manager at the expense of other social actors (e.g., the charismatic leader and/or the state/party administration) (Mihalyi 1992: 9; Earl, Frydman and Rapaczynski 1993: 5). In the Soviet block, these reforms progressed furthest in Hungary.

First, in 1968 the "New Economic Mechanism" voided the requirement for mandatory planning and resource allocation, obviously strengthening the property rights of firm-level actors. Then, from 1984–85, 70 percent of all enterprises were turned into self-governing entities with an elected manager or managerial body designated as leader.[3] The cumulative effect of these laws resulted in a transfer of "almost the entire bundle of property rights from the ministerial bodies to the enterprises themselves," and extended, to a significant degree, to the managers (Mihalyi 1992: 9; Voska 1994: 95). Even in Czechoslovakia, which was far more centralized than Hungary, the State-Owned Enterprise Act of 1987 vastly increased the scope of enterprise autonomy and, thereby, managers' property rights (Widmaier and Potratz 1996: 63).

It would not, therefore, be surprising for managers, in one or another manner, to utilize the different resources at their disposal during the transition to emerge as "winners." In each of the 50 firms I studied, managers used one or more of three types of resources. These resources were a monopoly of knowledge about their firm (see Widmaier and Potratz 1996: 67, for similar findings), their social capital (connections), and their human capital. This is not to say that managers "won" the game of transition in every case. Sometimes they were unsuccessful in their attempts to privatize, to restructure companies, or even to retain their own jobs. However, the general pattern that I found indicated a strong tendency toward finding solutions to the dilemmas of transition which rewarded some key group of higher-level management with money and/or ownership rights.

Other researchers have expressed similar opinions. For example, in Czechoslovakia,

It is beyond doubt that firm management had a great degree of control over the whole privatization process. Given the fact that management had an information monopoly on the elaboration of privatization projects and that managers are naturally the most familiar with the condition and productive capacities of their firms, it can be argued that firm management has more or less controlled the privatization process. These advantages were compounded by the fact that supervision of firms by branch ministries was very weak and the state planning agency was completely dismantled, so that there were no owners (i.e., government institutions) able to influence management. (Mejstrik 1995: 55)

Similarly, Szalai observes for Hungary that

In the power vacuum left by spontaneous privatization, corporate managers considerably increased their property rights at the expense of the state bureaucracy. (Szalai 1994: 124)

A small fraction of such activity is described as "management and employee buy-outs" by the formal assumption of share ownership. Many of the informal practices do not result in the firm structure and incentive structure expected by most economists. For example, the great insight of Szelenyi's managerialism thesis, which my research found to be completely accurate in some very significant and important instances (and always a useful theoretical hypothesis to guide empirical research), explains that managers would rather blur property rights than assume full or partial ownership (exactly the opposite of the "correct" set of property rights called for by economists), so as to receive the benefits of high wages without assuming the risky ownership of firms with an uncertain future.

My research demonstrates that there are a plurality of ways in which managers grab property rights—stemming from creating "correct" property rights in management buyouts, as well as by "blurring" rights as expected by Szelenyi, but also by creating alternative but "clear" types of property. In these latter types, ownership rights are clear (contra Szelenyi), and probably "correct" as well in terms of principal-agency efficiency arguments, although they do not conform to the Western distribution of property rights (contra the neoclassical economists). A striking example of this is MegaChem (auto-cross-ownership), discussed at length in chapter 2. This type of property consists of interlocking institutional ownership with interlocking directorates—such that an enterprise that employs 0.2 percent of the entire workforce of the Czech Republic is 85 percent owned, essentially, by itself. (Of the other 15 percent, roughly 10 percent is owned by the largest Czech Bank, which itself has significant government ownership, and the final 4.5 percent by employees and managers.)

MANAGERS AND EMPLOYEES

Before exploring the ways in which managers gain property rights, I must ask a more basic question: why structure the analysis around managers, as opposed to employees, or even manager-employee conflict? Burawoy, alone among the most important theorists of postcommunism, assigns a large causal role to the conflict and cooperation between employers and employees in explaining the transformation of the postcommunist firm. Burawoy argues that management abdicated control of the shop floor to the workers during socialism, and that this tendency has intensified in the postcommunist firm (Burawoy and Krotov 1992: 19). This worker control of the labor process forms a crucial element in his "merchant capitalism" thesis. Thus, the relationship between internal members of firms who collectively are owners—that is, the relationship between management and employees—must be examined. On the other hand, Burawoy's most recent formulations (1997) seem to be moving away from identifying this as the crucial element governing property transformation in Russia today.

I focus on management and managerial strategies, as opposed to focusing on employee ownership, for a complex set of reasons. The most important reason is due to the limitations of my data. Of the 50 firms I studied, only five had a major or majority ownership stake by workers. While the importance of managers as the real locus of property rights seemed to hold in these firms (although I did not interview regular workers, so even in these cases I lack an adequate basis for generalization), all five were in Slovenia, for which I am making no claims. Secondly, the statistical evidence does not allow me to consistently distinguish between employee and manager buy-outs. The 1993 Tarki data set allows me to get only a measure of manager and employee ownership. The 1996 Tarki data set fails to distinguish between manager buy-outs and other forms of private domestic ownership. My own mail survey, which allowed for this comparison, had only about 140 firms and a 30 percent response rate, greatly limiting its usefulness because of some low cell counts. Finally, in the little bit of direct evidence to this and related issues, I surmise that employee buy-outs (in conjunction with management buy-outs) are largely a hidden form of manager buy-outs.

For example, in the firms in my sample, employee representatives on supervisory boards in the Czech Republic are almost always from management (there was one case of a union boss serving on the board). This is confirmed by other researchers (for the Czech Republic see Widmaier and Potratz 1996: 69; for the Boards of Directors.[4] in Hungary see Karsai and Write 1994: 1007). Widmaier and Potratz base their findings on sectoral studies of the Czech canning, pharmaceutical and textile industries. In Mertlik's study of the Czech textile industry, he reports a manager saying

We (the managers of the textile and clothing companies) were invited to a meeting at the Ministry before privatization started and there a ministry official asked us who would like to be included in the first voucher privatization wave. Some of the managers raised their hands. And this was basically how some of the companies were included in to the first wave and the remaining to the later stages of the privatization process. (Mertlik 1995: 10)

In 17 case studies of manager and employee ownership in Hungary, Karsai and Write found that managers use employee buy-outs as a way to gain ownership:

In Hungary, the scope for buy-outs where management have a controlling interest has been constrained by an atmosphere of resistance to those company directors who were associated with the previous regime. Hence management could participate actively in privatization only as a complement to employee buy-outs. [Although this has changed since 1993, the authors go on to argue, as a result of the perception of many old managers being removed.] (Karsai and Write 1994: 1998)

As a result, "In most of the companies studied, management engaged in an active campaign to promote worker participation in the buy-out" (Karsai and Write 1994: 1005).

They go on to argue that managers basically run the show, although they do defer somewhat to employees over preserving employment.

One reason that managers enlist workers in buy-out schemes, no doubt, arises from the preferential terms granted to workers in the privatization process. For example, under the Hungarian ESOP law of 1992, employee buy-outs are financed with the so-called "existence" or "E-loan," and also receive a significant discount of shares. In practice, the benefits may be quite large indeed. For example, in Karsai and Write's study, they found that

When establishing the sale price, the State Property Agency granted without exception all the preferred terms and discounts available to workers in the Assets Policy Guidelines. In the case of employees' shares the discount could reach as high as 90 percent, compared with a general entitlement to a 50 percent discount, with the remaining portion of the assets normally offered at the nominal price. (Karsai and Write 1994: 1003)

These discounts were set by size of assets, and "the proportion of the annual gross basic pay accounted for by the purchasing collective" (1003).

In my own research I came across some highly subsidized management buy-outs. VeggieCo. had been the state-owned company that produced and distributed vegetable seeds in Slovakia. It was privatized in 1995, one month prior to my interview with the former manager, director and biggest owner. VeggieCo. was owned completely by its top five managers. The terms of the buy-out seemed pretty generous. The payments for the company were to be made over ten years.

In the first three years, all payments went into reinvestment in the company. After this, the firm is expected to pay back the loan from its profits. VeggieCo.'s new owners made their first payment not from their own money, however, but from their turnover. This "payment" went to purchasing a machine from Holland that upgraded the packaging of their seeds. This management buy-out strategy seemed to be combined with a political capitalist strategy, demonstrating once again that in many cases there is not a single strategy employed, but rather a combination of strategies.

The CEO admitted the privatization was quite a bargain. Where the company had a book value of 39 million crowns (about 1.3 million USD), the final privatization contract (with the extremely favorable payment scheme described above) was for only seven million Slovak crowns. When I asked how he accounted for this, he told me "don't ask how it was so. You need the right person, at the right time, in the right place to privatize." It seemed that this company was also able to benefit from subterranean redistribution, as it received subsidies of 30 percent from the government for buying seeds, chemistry tools and equipment, and another 30 to 35 percent for the costs of developing new breeds.

While property can sometimes be acquired quite cheaply by managers, especially when done in conjunction with employee ownership, all commentators and researchers report (or assert) that managers then go on to dominate in the new "employee-owned" firms:

There have been suggestions that employee buy-outs in Hungary are typically controlled by management. In many firms the opportunity to subscribe for shares was typically limited by a set of rules which tended to mean that managers and long-serving employees obtained the highest amount of shares. The subscription quota for individual workers was determined by a system of points reflecting the number of years at the company, position and income. (Karsai and Write 1994: 1005)

And, if seniority is not the principal determinant of share distribution, then money is, which obviously also favors management. In CzechPress, discussed in chapter 2, the CEO told me that the managers completely dominated the legally mandated process by which workers appoint one-third of the seats on the Supervisory Board. The chief economists of the Hungarian State Property Agency told me that it was "common knowledge" that managers dominated employee buy-outs. Moreover, my fieldwork shows that, over time, managers tend to buy shares from employees, as was the case with MegaChem as discussed in chapter 2. This was also the case at all five firms where I did fieldwork in Slovenia.

Furthermore, the diffuse ownership among employees, as well as the managerial monopolization of information (again according to fairly preliminary data) further strengthened managers relative to workers. Thus, in Hungary

Employee-owners were typically, because of their low and diffuse equity stakes together with lack of expertise, unable to exercise an effective supervisory role. Moreover, employees were presented with insufficient information with which to exercise control, either in terms of proper representation or a system of weekly and monthly reports. Feasibility studies and business plans were neither detailed nor concrete enough to make these documents suitable for exerting some sort of external control. (Karsai and Write 1994: 1007)

Indeed, employees "with their generally low equity stakes, did not see themselves as owners. As the proportion of their incomes made up by dividends was insignificant, the focus of employees' attention was on receiving higher wages and keeping their jobs" (1007). While these findings are based on only 17 firms, this represents the most direct evidence collected to date, at least in the secondary literature I read (which includes nearly everything written in English on the subject).

The ownership structure that results from management and employee buy-outs usually favors a group of core managers. Among the 17 firms studied by Karsai and Write, "typically 15–25 managers in each firm obtained significant if not controlling ownership stakes. Typically a relatively small management group held a majority stake or a stake in excess of 25%, ensuring management's power of veto. The equity stake held by employees, even where it was large, was typically diffused across many workers" (1006).

In my own research, there were indeed groups of managers that collectively controlled the firm. This was the case at CzechPress, discussed in chapter 2, as well as at others to be detailed later in this chapter. Indeed, one striking observation in my research was the seeming absence of any significant class struggle between workers and managers/owners. There were several strikes during my research stay, but these were primarily in the state service sector. (In my eight months of fieldwork there were strikes or threats of strikes by teachers, transport workers, and doctors.) Only one manager in my study reported having any problem with employees, and this firm was in a position of extremely attenuated ownership by banks and passive investment companies, and was riddled with parasitic satellite companies created by former managers.

For the most part, according to what I could observe (although again I didn't interview employees), and to what others have written on the subject, the employees depend on management to run the company, especially in interfirm relations. Still, this dominance of managers over employees was not absolute. According to Karsai and Write, "management appeared to recognize the importance of maintaining employees' acceptance of their position. Hence, pressures by management to reduce employment levels as part of restructuring were moderated" (1011). Nonetheless, in my sample of manager-owned firms, significant (and in some cases massive) labor reduction occurred.

A TYPOLOGY OF MANAGERIAL ACTIVITY TO GAIN PROPERTY RIGHTS

As stated, postcommunist managers have employed a variety of strategies to transform the postcommunist firm and economy, as well as to transform themselves from state-appointed bureaucrats into a property-owning class or a managerial elite that controls firms. These are:

1. Simple management and employee buy-outs
2. Leasing arrangements
3. Cross-ownership buy-outs

4. Satellite firms funneling firm assets

5. Simple self-ownership

6. Auto-cross-ownership

Table 5.2 summarizes the property rights that come to managers given the different strategies.

Table 5.2
Strategies of Managerialization

Strategy	Insiders' Property Rights		
	Income	*Control*	*Transfer*
Manager and employee buy-outs	all	all	all
Cross-management buy-outs	all	all	all
Leases	some	all	none
Satellites	a lot	a lot	none
Simple self-ownership	some	most	a little
Auto-cross ownership	all	all	all

SIMPLE MANAGEMENT AND EMPLOYEE BUY-OUTS

This is a strategy in which a group of managers, often with the cooperation of workers, privatize the original state-owned enterprise (or a division of such an enterprise). This is typically accomplished by forming a limited liability company that privatizes the original company. We have already seen two examples of this: [BudaLamp (discussed in Chapter 4) and VeggicCo. (discussed in this chapter). The secondary literature discussed also refers to this type of activity.

The 1993 Tarki survey of 1000 firms only allows for the identification of manager- and employee-owned firms. One can not tell the proportions of each— only the amount owned by the manager who is the interviewee (usually the CEO). Of these, 22.6 percent of the largest 3000 firms in 1992 were at least 30 percent– owned by managers and employees. As expected, these firms are smaller than firms having other types of ownership. Table 5.3 shows that manager- and/or employee-owned firms are overrepresented among smaller firms; the larger the firm, the less likely manager and/or employee ownership becomes.

Appendix 8 shows in what sectors of the Hungarian economy manager- and/or employee-owned firms (MEBOs) are located. We see that, although there are many MEBOs in industry (about 73 out of 404 total), MEBOs are significantly underrepresented in this sector. Undoubtedly, this is partially a result of the large average size of industrial firms, which makes them more expensive for managers

Table 5.3
Size of Management and Employee Buy-outs

Number of employees	MEBO less than 30% ownership	MEBO at least 30% ownership	Total
less than 100	72.2%	27.8%	526
101 to 300	75.6%	24.4%	234
301 to 1000	88.7%	11.3%	177
1001 to 3000	94.1%	5.9%	51
more than 3000	100.0%	0.0%	13
Total number of firms	775	226	1001
Percent of total	77.4%	22.6%	100.0%

to purchase. MEBOs are also more likely in agriculture. There is evidence that these MEBOs may be combined with a satellite strategy to unload debt on the state (see Havas, Ladanyi and Szelenyi 1996).

Another interesting finding is the unexpected lack of overrepresentation in the commerce sector—in opposition to Staniszkis's theory as detailed above. Managers do not seem to be disproportionately inserting themselves into the "sphere of circulation." Perhaps there are many smaller commercial firms that are dominated by former managers. These firms would typically be quite little, Staniszkis could reasonably argue, and the examples from LuxTrade in my field-work support this position. So, the final verdict on this particular thesis of Staniszkis' must remain uncertain until better evidence is found.

Also relevant to this point is the fact that MEBOs are not disproportionately staffed by former members of the Communist Party, as we would expect if Staniszkis' description of cadre firms holds at all for the Hungarian context (at least of relatively large firms). (The percentage of the questionnaire respondents of MEBOs who reported former membership in the Workers' Party is 21.9—the difference from the expected proportion (22.6%) is not even close to significant.) We also know that these firms are disproportionately spinoffs from cooperatives, and thus disproportionately not from state companies or joint-stock companies (see Appendix 1).

Perhaps the most interesting finding is that these firms are disproportionately more profitable than non-MEBOs, as shown in Table 5.4.

MEBOs are much more likely than non-MEBOs to have very high levels of profitability. One can only wonder at the cause of this, as the finding is fairly unexpected given the very high debt payments these firms supposedly must make. On the other hand, the efficiency advantages of internalizing principal-agent externalities may be responsible for these very high levels of profits. The other likely cause gleaned from my fieldwork suggests that MEBOs as a strategy are

Table 5.4
Profitability by Management and/or Employee Buy-outs

	MEBO less than 30% ownership	MEBO at least 30% ownership	Total
No profits	79.1%	20.9%	492
0–10%	81.8%	18.2%	335
10–20%	70.6%	29.4%	68
20–50%	61.5%	38.5%	65
50+%	58.5%	41.5%	41
Total number of firms	775	226	1001
Percent of total	77.4%	22.6%	100.0%

often combined with satellite strategies that result in the unloading of unproductive assets on the state—which should create quite profitable firms.

Another interesting finding is that MEBOs seem to operate in a slightly less statist part of the economy, and seem to be overrepresented among firms that are heavily dependent on domestic sources of inputs as well as domestic markets for their sales. In Appendix 11, *state dependence* measures the proportion of the firm's total inputs and sales that comes from state budgets. In Appendix 10, *domestic dependence* measures the proportion of the total inputs and sales that are dependent on domestic as opposed to foreign sources. A low score represents less than or equal to 10 percent of all inputs and outputs coming from a source, a medium score represents more than 10 percent and less than 30 percent, a high score represents more than 30 and less than 50 percent, and a very high score means more than 50 percent. Appendix 11 demonstrate that MEBOs are slightly overrepresented among firms whose state dependence is low, and underrepresented among very highly state-dependent firms. Appendix 11 shows that MEBOs are highly overrepresented among those firms that buy more than 50 percent of their inputs from, and sell more than 50 percent of their outputs to, domestically owned firms (state and private).

I also have some data on the pervasiveness of clientelism among the management- and/or employee-owned firms. The data show that the respondents (usually the CEO or other high-level managers) of MEBO firms disproportionately report regularly "getting the help from a friend or relation" in obtaining credit, making purchases, getting sales, and receiving help with the custom office. On the other hand, the data also show that the respondents at these firms disproportionately report that they do not have connections to the Ministry of Finance (see Appendix 9). It could be that manager-owners are typically very well-connected individuals who use these clientelistic connections to their advantage—and that it is the larger firms, less likely to be subject to a MEBO, which are connected to the Ministry of Finance. On the other hand, I think one should be extremely cautious about making any inference about the actual extent of clientelism from a survey questionnaire like this one, so too much should not be made of these last findings.

LEASES

Manager and/or employee buy-outs which result in the formal assumption of property rights are not the only method by which firm insiders move to gain property. The purchase of shares by firm insiders is usually done at a discount, as has been detailed. Still, there remain groups that are quite hard-pressed to obtain the money for a buy-out. In some such cases, managers may lease the property for some time, possibly with the intention of buying it later. This was definitely the case with the one lease in my sample. Unfortunately, I have not come across any solid empirical analysis on leases—just newspaper reports. This form may arise when the local managers are in a strong position to purchase and restructure the enterprises (or they are the only ones interested), but they do not have the money to do the job, or do not want to privatize some or most of the enterprise's debt or old capital stock.

Leases have the obvious disadvantage of making the debt problem discussed even worse. Indeed, in one respect, leases can be viewed as similar to a bank loaning an employee/management group money to do a buy-out—except that the rights held by a major debtor (and these usually include the right to place an appointee on the Supervisory Board) are strengthened. However, the property rights accruing to the manager are much more partial under leasing arrangements. While managers have a large amount of control over the enterprise, managers' rights to residual income are extremely curtailed, and they do not have the right to sell their property at all. The data needed to determine the long-term future of most leases are lacking, although I suspect most leases will eventually be bought out.

The one example of leasing in my fieldwork involves a factory located in Bratislava. TESLA Electronics was transformed in 1995 into a state factory under liquidation. As will be detailed, this company had accrued significant debt over the last four to five years. As the CEO—the most important "lessee" and my interviewee—explained, the government extended these loans because, as a result of the disintegration of the COMECON market, which made up almost the entire market for this firm's most important product (public address systems), the business would have been plunged into bankruptcy. He suggested that the government could not destroy the factory overnight, leaving everyone unemployed at once, so they did it step by step. This tendency to slow down or prevent bankruptcies in order to dampen the shock of the transition was examined in chapter 2 in the discussion on "subterranean redistribution."

Thus, for the first four to five years, the government gave loans to this state-owned enterprise at 20 to 30 percent interest. The CEO thought the government would keep giving these loans, which seemed to be extended automatically. Indeed, the CEO did not even know which banks extended the loans. He only knew they were "connected to the government." The bank took stock and real estate as collateral. Eventually, the company had so many loans that it was liquidated by the bank. A new limited liability company was formed by the managers of this and a closely related firm—which received a lease for TESLA.

The interviewee—the CEO and one of the core owners of the limited liability company that owns the lease to TESLA—wants eventually to buy the company outright. The group of manager/owners is in a struggle with the bank over the terms of the buy-out. The CEO hoped that this struggle would be won through political channels. The CEO pointed out that his firm's primary political asset was its 200 workers who were not yet unemployed.[5]

The CEO explained that he believed he would eventually obtain the right to purchase the company, although if someone else made a bid they might win that right, but only if they would guarantee that they will keep the old employees. From the way the interviewee talked about the lease, it was obviously an interface for the struggle over property rights, in particular the right to residual income or profit.

Interestingly, and tellingly, while the CEO looked to the government, or the "state," for the solution to his firm's problems, he also looked at the "state" as the problem—underscoring the point made in chapter 2 about government ownership being less than its numerical representation might indicate. That is, the "state" as a concept in postcommunism is only useful at a very high degree of generalization—the "state" usually consists of various organizations which may well have conflicting agendas and different types and amounts of power.

In the words of the interviewee, "The man here from the government—he is a big pig—he only wants to suck money from the company." This "big pig" is the man who administers the lease from the Ministry of the Economy for TESLA. This underscores the extent to which manager's rights to residual income is limited by the leasing body of the government.

Each month his limited liability company must pay the lease five days in advance. This lease is an enormous part of their expenses. For example, salaries, including the 38 percent for insurance and taxes, are 1.7 million SK per, while the lease alone is 1.2 million SK! Obviously, as the CEO pointed out, this money could be used to buy inputs, not to mention restructuring or training. So he says he wants to buy as soon as possible. In 1995 they promised he could buy in December, which was pushed back to January, then February, and now the summer.

The interviewee offered the insight that it was not in the interest of the liquidator, the particular bureaucrat, to approve the sale of the firm. He was appointed from the Ministry, and only gets a check so long as he is "administering" the lease. Thus, the interviewee bluntly told me that he searches for connections over this man. He explained that the Ministry of the Economy is internally torn over what to do with his firm. "There are lots of departments in the ministry—one appoints the liquidator—the other department wants to see these people keep their jobs." He was confident he would resolve this issue of property through political means. He felt that if he could only get directly to Meciar, and past the levels of bureaucrats, he could get action. He explained that to get to Meciar you must take all the steps on the ladder to obtain the right papers, saying the problem cannot be solved at the lower levels.

The lease, in this case at least, was a crystallization of struggles over property rights. For example, the interviewee said the management group had a privatization plan all approved, only the state insisted on saddling the company with its bad debts. So he prefers to buy from the liquidator, who holds the title to the entire property. He will buy only the buildings, grounds and machines they use. Thus the lease, if my interviewee gets his way, will perform the function that the "satellite" firms do—it would provide an avenue for the privatizing of assets and the socializing of costs. This experience raises the interesting question of whether this process—from the enclosure movement 500 years ago in England to the creation of satellite companies in Prague in the 1990s—is generic in "transitions" to capitalism.

The firm TESLA Electronics not only provides insight into an important new type of property relationship, "leases," but also provides an example of a buy-out as an attempt by the CEO to pursue a strategy of cross-management ownership.

CROSS-MANAGEMENT OWNERSHIP

This strategy consists of managers gaining property rights by creating an arrangement between groups of managers in firms that have cooperated extensively in the past. In my one example of this behavior, TESLA, the managers from each group formed a limited liability company that collectively leased their companies.

This company, specializing in the production of professional audio equipment, was founded in 1939 by the German company Telefunken. At first the firm only repaired broadcasting equipment made in Germany. During the war the company stayed independent and produced military equipment for the German Republic with 20 to 30 employees. The factory was physically destroyed in the final year of the war when there was fighting on Slovakian soil. After the war Czechoslovakia was re-established with the help of the Red Army. The new government reconstructed the company, and it grew very quickly until it was nationalized in 1948.

The CEO described the firm, where he has worked since 1958, as a small, highly skilled and specialized factory with between 100 and 200 employees. In 1958 there was a world exhibition in Brussels for public sound equipment. This company, which made the audio equipment for the famed "Laterna Magica" theater in Prague, entered miniaturized equipment which was awarded first prize in its class. They developed the miniaturization technology themselves, and it soon became the model others would follow.

This feat caught the eye of those planning the Soviet Union's merciless industrialization drive, and a massive expansion of the company resulted when planners in the Soviet Union decided Communism needed the equipment that won first prize in Brussels.

Following this event they built another factory, but this still wasn't enough expansion to meet the Soviet Union's demand. The company kept growing, and by 1989 there were 1,600 employees, up from 150 in 1960. The factory continued producing professional audio equipment for radio, television, theaters, and public address systems. They were the clear leader for this product in the Soviet block.

TESLA sold predominantly to the Soviet Union, and they had no Western markets at all. As the interviewee pointed out, this occurred because Western countries bought domestically made equipment for security reasons (although he claimed that German companies came to their firm to see their techniques).

Because of their almost complete dependence on the COMECON market, and the Soviet Union in particular, the transition from Communism was a catastrophe for this company. In 1991 they exported nothing to the Soviet Union. From 1600 employees they shrunk to between 350 and 400 employees in 1995, and then to only 200 in 1996. Again, the interviewee expressed hope that he could convince the government to provide an infusion of cash into the company. Since, as he explained, "the politicians destroyed their markets," they should help them get new ones. However, the attempt to use "political capital," that is, the social capital embodied in connections to members of state bureaucracies, is not an exclusive strategy, and is not necessarily inimical to entrepreneurial activity and market-adaptive strategies. In fact, given the adoption of this strategy by other firms, such behavior can easily be construed as rational.

The CEO of TESLA explained that Germany, the logical new customer for their products, became instead the home of their fiercest competitor. Siemens, the giant German multinational, was busy trying to take over the Slovak market. As is characteristic of many firms in much of the region, TESLA has been forced to move toward lower-tech, low-value-added activities to stay alive, substituting technical superiority for the advantages of close proximity to Western Europe and cheap labor.

TESLA now makes electronic equipment like irons and lights. This production is essentially assembly work. However, they still have a significant number of people, 35 out of 200 employees, in the research and development department, working on personal computers. In the CEO's search for new products he met with over a hundred businessmen from the West, which resulted in several strong partnerships. Partly funded by the PHARE program, they make irons with an Italian partner, which he claims is a better deal for the Italian partner than for his company. The second partner is a German who imports nightclub-style lights for discos and restaurants and distributes them throughout Western Europe. The third new partner is a company from Holland that also specializes in bulk mechanical parts for electronics. Finally, the CEO has reestablished some of his company's markets for broadcast equipment in the former Soviet Union, primarily in the Ukraine and Russia.

As has been noted above, the company was leased by a limited liability company. There was no Board of Directors, only direct meetings of the seven domestic owners of the two limited liability companies. This ownership pattern results in a unique ownership form: cross-ownership management buy-outs.

The "real" ultimate owner of this group of three companies, therefore, is the Ministry of Finance. That is, the Ministry and the group of seven managers share rights to residual income, while the Ministry has rights to sell the property and the managers have the right to organize production. Thus, if the CEO and his co-owner/managers are successful, the two firms will be completely owned by the seven managers from two firms that had long cooperated in the Communist period.

The video company does engineering for videos and has only 15 employees. Their production facility is physically located in the factory and grounds of TESLA. The two companies, which still draw up production plans with each other, collectively owned another company—the 400-employee East Slovakian daughter company—which was also liquidated. Together, these seven people will essentially control all the significant ownership rights in the three firms, employing about 415 people, providing they manage to buy out the lease.

Interestingly, although the very existence of this property form is predicated on a lease, the resulting company, at least in this case, was not able to draw on clientelistic networks to get loans. If we remember from the previous section on leasing that I hypothesize that this lease is a crystallization of struggle, and at the same time a mechanism for the successful claim on the companies' profits, it is perhaps not surprising that this firm is starved for lack of investment capital. They simply did not take loans and invested only their own money.

Thus, while previously they were arguably a world leader in the production of public announcement equipment (tested, furthermore, in the flames of competition with companies from other East block countries, from a demanding purchaser, which resulted in years of accumulated specialized high-tech know-how), they have been surviving primarily by shifting to the production of low-tech electronic assembly. Given their dire financial straits, this is understandable, and seems like the most rational and viable option. However, when aggregated across the economy, this business strategy results in an overall long-term disastrous erosion of the postcommunist base of human capital, the cheap but relatively skilled and educated workforce which should be their natural "comparative advantage" that drives these economies to close the gap between themselves and Western Europe.

The experience of TESLA, unfortunately, may not be an isolated incident. According to Widmaier and Potratz, based on a study of firms in 18 industries in six countries (three industries per country), they find that "Changes in product structure show a general tendency towards less sophisticated products" in Eastern Europe (1996: 15).

This case of managerial buy-out is instructive in one final way—in terms of a class theory of the transition from socialism to capitalism. The managers that led this restructuring are indeed the very same actors whom Szelenyi and his collaborators point out as the embodiment of new class formation in late socialism—the meeting point of the *telos* of socialism with the *techne* of scientific rationality.

In 1968 the interviewee belonged to the Communist Party, an ardent supporter of Dubcek at the age of 34. He said he was one of the "progressives, who wanted to mix socialism with capitalism, like they are doing in China." After the invasion of Czechoslovakia, the interviewee was demoted from his position of firm director to a bottom-level position where, as he put it, he experienced twenty hard years. He kept his job as a researcher and invented a process which formed the basis of the East Slovakian sister company, which at its height employed 500 people. As a result of this, he was again promoted to a technical position, although he was not allowed back in management or the Party. Forbidden to travel in the Soviet Union, he was allowed to go West. Thus, as Szelenyi argued, even the neo-Stalinist Czech regime was forced to increase the importance of expertise in selecting people for promotion. Indeed, Mertlik (1995) claims that by the mid-1980s membership in the Communist Party was almost purely symbolic, and a massive amount of cynicism regarding Communism existed among the technoc racy and managerial elite.

SATELLITE FIRMS FUNNELING ASSETS TO MANAGERS

Management buy-outs and cross-owned management buy-out groups all involved the former appropriation of the entire bundle of property rights of some former state-owned company or part of a state-owned company. This activity, however important, is only one part of the total economic activity associated with managers transforming state property in postcommunist society. Leases are an important, if relatively unexplored, form of property in which property rights remain divided between managers and some state institution. Equally interesting is the appropriation of "property," broadly conceived, from state-owned firms via satellite firms owned by managers, as discussed in chapter 2.

Walters (1990), a personal advisor to Thatcher, wrote that the transformation of the postcommunist economy "can be broadly characterized as the existing management's stealing the capital and running off with it." Nuti (1990) likens the process to very bad insider trading. According to Mejstrik, the

Management of state-owned firms often took advantage of its position to strip assets to cover operating losses and provide themselves with increased income. Also, managers were able to set up parallel companies and use transfer prices to sell products almost at a loss to the private companies they owned, thus transferring large profits to themselves. These practices could even in some cases lead to bankruptcy of the state-owned company, which could then be cheaply acquired by the new, liquid private company. (Mejstrik 1995: 56)

Voska sees a similar process in Hungary: "Managers seem to have enhanced their incomes more through transfer pricing arrangements than through asset-grabbing" (1993: 106).

Staniszkis also describes this type of activity, grouping it with other forms of "political capitalism." In her discussion of economic change in Poland, Staniszkis sees the emergence of "political capitalism" in which the old *nomenklatura* become the owners of firms in trade and production relying on "various combinations of power and capital" for their survival and expansion (1991: 38). By virtue of their political capital, they are able to insert themselves in the sphere of circulation of capital and make a profit. These firms: "link capital and markets of various kinds which otherwise would not come into contact because of the rules of the game or which are still isolated from one another by a buffer zone and thus can be approached only by those companies because the authorities regard such mediation as beneficial" (38).

These firms may act "as brokers in the export of products of state enterprises to capitalist markets replacing state foreign trade offices" (39), or set up "small cooperative companies . . . to act as middlemen between state enterprises and the traditional private sector" (40). Thus, "In this brokerage activity the 'basic capital' is access to information and means of transportation; being in the nomenclature affords both" (41).

It bears repeating that the above formulations may well only be "common wisdom," as none of the authors presented anything more than anecdotes as evidence. Nonetheless, it must at least be a strong hypothesis that managers are able to do this, and indeed I found a great deal of evidence in my fieldwork that this strategy was being used.

I was struck by the number of "satellite" firms that I ran into in my fieldwork (others have called them "parallel companies" or "buy-pass companies"). Some of these forms were discussed in chapter 2. One type, which I call "short-term parasitic companies" (see the example of the Czech Travel Agency in chapter 2), was fairly widespread.

Short-Term Satellites

I saw a surprising amount of satellite creation in all three countries in my study, even if much of it seemed to net the managers trivial amounts of money. In chapter 2, I detailed the example of managers forming companies for imaginary work in the travel business in the Czech state tourist company prior to its privatization. I found the exact same story from an interview with the Slovak equivalent. Many managers funneled funds out of the mother company to themselves via the creation of subcontracting companies.

While "mimetic isomorphism" (Dimagio and Powell 1983) may have had an effect in this case (one would expect the managers of one state travel company to be watching and imitating the behavior of the other state travel company), it is also likely that this strategy is selected in very big companies, still owned by the state, but undergoing what Mertlik calls "pre-privatization agony" (1996)—the radical uncertainty of not knowing who the owners will be or what business plans they will implement.

Economists have a useful theoretical construct for explaining this behavior: principal-agent theory. Where the agents (the managers) exist in a situation of very weak, probably temporary, and disorganized ownership with almost no power to supervise or monitor them, it is in the agents interest to obtain a little "insurance" against an uncertain future by paying themselves for nothing.

There were other examples of "satellite creation" which were more significant. For example, the Slovak firm VeggieCo. previously discussed experienced this. This state monopoly for seed production and distribution once had 1500 to 2000 people in various branches of the company and in 12 retail shops. From 1990 until July 1994, the companies separated. The first to separate were the ones being liquidated, thus unloading the least valuable property onto the state. According to the owner/CEO, the worthless property was liquidated at no cost to the managers, and then "each manager wanted to be independent, so they split up the rest."

This fragment of the old company, now owned by five managers and employing 100 people, has 20 to 25 percent of the domestic market in vegetable seeds for small consumers who mostly do gardening as a hobby. They market their seeds in the twelve shops they still own throughout Slovakia (along with other gardening supplies) and sell wholesale as well.

The director and owner explained a situation in which a fairly significant "satellite" seems to have been formed. Since 1992 the company has been in court because of happenings at a branch of the company that was separated and privatized in 1992 under the Small Privatization Act. The company got a loan of 100 million SK to pay for privatization, which they never repaid. According to the interviewee, all stock and workers disappeared overnight, leaving an empty building sitting on property they illegally sold (thus the court case). The interviewee was visibly upset at this recollection as he pointed out the window at the rusted iron roof of a large and crude adjacent building, bitter at the loss of his firm's assets.

Long-Term Satellites

Thus short-term parasitic companies, formed by managers, allow for the appropriation of capital. This type of short-term satellite creation can be distinguished from the long-term variety of this strategy, wherein the managers form parasitic satellites that persist over time, in one way or another constantly taking the "host" firm's assets or profits. In the second chapter, I presented the case study of FoodCo. to illustrate this process.

Another example of a relatively small long-term parasitic satellite was in the Hungarian firm HungDrugs. This company existed for 150 years as many small druggeries. The Hungarian state nationalized them fifty years ago, and since 1993 they have been in a prolonged process of privatization. The firm has mixed ownership, which is broken down in Table 5.5.

Table 5.5
Ownership Structure of HungDrugs

Owner	Share
Private individuals	52%
State property agency	22–25%
Local government	8–11%
Employee ownership group	15%

(Three percent of the State Property Agency shares are to be transferred to the local government as the result of a lawsuit.)

The Board of Directors consists of five people—the three largest private investors, and the last two directors of the firm. It seems that the most important owner is a limited liability company. This company is run by a very rich private Hungarian who had been a chairman of a major sporting union. Others in the limited liability company were old managers "who helped in the privatization," altogether about 15 people. Still, three people have 90 percent of all the shares, and according to my interviewee "they decide things over dinner before the meetings." When I asked the interviewee about satellite companies, he acknowledged that some of the owners did own businesses, and that satellites were a problem, but he "didn't want to get into it." But, he pointed out, much as Marx did in *Das Kapital* when considering "primitive accumulation," this was "one step in the development of capitalism, a necessary bad thing." You need capitalists to have capitalism, and legally it can't be done." He even informed me that two-thirds of the British Parliament stole their fortunes in an attempt to normalize this behavior to me. One example he gave was of a company founded by the major owner and CEO himself, which contracts with HungDrugs for 5 million HUF (about US $40,000) a year to "supplement" his salary, an amount the State Property Agency and other owners would find excessive and unacceptable.

One can compare this phenomenon with Szelenyi's managerialism thesis. The interviewee from HungDrugs went on to make a remark that was consonant with Szelenyi's theory, "if the water is too clear, muddy it." Thus, because of the very complicated and mixed nature of property, the managers were able to expand their own wealth without taking, necessarily, the costs and risks of ownership. However, this was actually a stealing of resources, which somewhat contradicts the early managerialism theory as advanced thus far by Szelenyi.

While the amount stolen by the CEO of HungDrugs is relatively small, long-term satellites can be far more devastating. LuxTrade, like FoodCo. and MegaChem, had the Czechoslovakian state monopoly on various imported luxury goods. During Communism these shops allowed Communist elites to spend special credits, which they exchanged for hard currency they accumulated abroad, on certain high-quality consumer goods unavailable to the rest of the population, such as imported scotch and fine cigars. As a result of its long history, LuxTrade has many outlets and excellent name recognition. LuxTrade was a state-owned enterprise until the first wave of privatization. It is a typical large "private" Czech enterprise, with the majority of shares in institutional ownership, in which the owners are investment companies owned by banks or other financial institutions that are in turn majority-owned by the State. This ownership structure is detailed in Table 5.6.

After privatization, according to my interviewee, control was dispersed and did not function very well. The representatives of the owning investment funds did not have any expertise with foreign trade. He joined the company in March of 1995 because of the resulting bad situation.

He explained that members of the Board of Directors get special payment for coming to the meetings. He said that in the last four years none of the owners took an interest in running the firm or in providing leadership or strategy. The members of the Board were lower-level employees of the investment funds, who did not know anything about the business and did not really care about it. He said "They give some stupid advice—and I give them lots of materials on the business which they don't even bother to read."

This type of "absentee" ownership creates just those principal-agent problems predicted by economic theory. Again, we get a large company with no clear supervision or monitoring by owners. My interviewee, the General Director and Chairman of the Board, explained to me a situation that sounds very much like Jadigwa Staniszkis' description of manager-owned satellite companies making money by inserting themselves in the sphere of trade.

According to the interviewee, after privatization, when there was no real control, the old managers of LuxTrade set up independent companies that signed exclusive rights for various items, bought them wholesale from the West, and then resold them to LuxTrade, taking 80 percent of the margin in the process.

Thus, LuxTrade went from being a state monopoly to being the launching pad of tiny parasitic mini-monopolists for certain specific luxury commodities (like RayBan sunglasses, scotch, and so on). These firms add nothing to production, nor do they make the Czech market any less monopolistic. Their parasitism is predicated on the existence of the huge chain of distributors and name recognition of the mother company (or more accurately the host company). They take the

Table 5.6
Ownership Structure of LuxTrade

Owner	Share
Investment fund of State Trading Bank	30%
Investment fund of Czech Insurance	11%
Investment fund of Czech Savings Bank	7%
Investment fund of Czech Commercial Bank	7%
A private investment fund	7%
Individual voucher holders	38%

profit out of the company, sucking it dry not only of funds for innovation, but even of money to buy new goods.

SIMPLE SELF-OWNERSHIP AND AUTO-CROSS-OWNERSHIP

The final ways in which managers gain property rights in their old firms involve the creative use of institutional ownership to maintain management control against possible outside owners (such as the State, outside investors, private individuals, or foreign companies). In the example of CzechPress in chapter 2, we saw how managers, by becoming partial owners of their own company, were able to split the power of outside owners and thereby maintain insider control of the supervisory board. In the MegaChem example, we see how cross-institutional ownership creates a form of property in which the top managers of the companies within the business group are collectively able to gain the entire bundle of property rights.

These diverse strategies of "managerialization" are listed in Table 5.7. In this table, what is "privatized" is specified, as is the resulting form of property.

Table 5.7
Strategies of Managerialization and the Resulting Type of Property

Strategy by Managers	*What is Privatized Property*	*Type of Resulting*
MEBOs	The entire bundle of property rights	Western-style MEBO
Cross-owned buy-outs	The entire bundle of property rights	Cross-ownership
Leases	Control rights, some rights to residual income	State-ownership
Short-term satellites	Wealth	Parasitic structure
Long-term satellites	Some residual income, some control	Parasitic structure
Simple self-ownership	The right to control some residual income some rights to sell	Manager self-ownership
Auto-cross-ownership	The entire bundle of property rights	Private ownership without private owners

CONCLUSION

We see that analysis of manager and employee buy-outs must move beyond paying exclusive attention to the legal attainment of ownership rights, to examine various informal processes as well. Indeed, the already significant formal ownership of managers, combined with the other ways in which managers acquire property and/or property rights, characterizes a major (and perhaps dominant) proportion of the types of firm transformations present in the postcommunist economies. More research is needed to fully understand this issue.

I have no systematic data on managers' motivations and reasoning, but one can theorize that the strategy that managers employ depends on the specific circumstances they find themselves in at the time of privatization. Clearly, as Table 5.3 makes abundantly clear, a very important variable is the size of the enterprise. In my fieldwork, I found the presence or absence of a strong owner capable of monitoring managers to be equally important. Where the firm is inexpensive enough (and thus the importance of size), managers have an easier time buying a controlling share in the firm. Or, they might temporarily lease this firm, hoping to buy it (or its liquidated assets) some day. When the firm has no strong owner and/or poor supervision by owners, managers are able to use satellite firms to funnel resources out of the firms and into their own hands. When the specific ownership configuration makes it possible, managers may also attempt to employ auto-cross-ownership strategies—this is likely a legacy of legal peculiarities (e.g., MegaChem's unusual ownership structure at the time of privatization, a contingent event resulting from reforms in 1968). The likely economic and developmental effects of the different strategies of managerialization will be discussed in chapter 6.

NOTES

1. Of course, some argue that this discriminates against those in the public sector, who would have no chance of becoming an owner.

2. Of course, it is a tradition of economic sociology that perfectly regulating markets never exist anywhere, and in fact the closer a society is to perfect markets, the more politically unstable that society will be (see Polanyi's classic statement on this [1944/1957]).

3. This was more than half the value of all state assets (Mihalyi 1992: 9).

4. In the Czech Republic the Supervisory Board is usually the most powerful body (as in the German system, although a mix of the American and German systems is also emerging), whereas in Hungary the Board of Directors is usually the supreme organ (as in the Anglo-American tradition).

5. Indeed, this is the first person I had heard talk about Mcciar in a positive light. Most intellectuals who despise Meciar for his authoritarian proclivities infrequently mention that his appeal lies to a large extent in his monopolization of the position in the political field that, at least in rhetoric, most consistently seeks to protect Slovakian workers, primarily by protecting their jobs.

6

Conclusion: The Emergence of Capitalism in Postcommunist Eastern Europe

This chapter, the conclusion to my book, will do more than simply summarize my findings. It will also speculate on the future of capitalism in Hungary and the former Czechoslovakia, and identify areas for future research.

How, then, to conclude my argument? This study of the postcommunist firm in Central Europe was intended to partially answer the following interrelated set of questions: (1) What are the most important ways agents "make capitalism" in Eastern Europe? By what methods and means has state-owned property been transformed, and new firms created, over the last eight years or so? (2) Has a capitalist economy developed? If so, what kind of capitalist economy is it?

In the preceding three chapters I provided a description of the transformation of firms, and their current structure of property rights and organization. I have described many "strategies" that are not typically thought of as "capitalist" or "market oriented." The most significant of these activities are securing resources from the state (what I call "subterranean redistribution"), using clientelistic relationships between firms and sources of finance, using political connections or power to secure profits, and using satellite firms to systematically funnel resources out of firms. All of these activities are nonmarket mechanisms that in a "pure" capitalist system (according to theory) would be carried out in self-regulating markets. Furthermore, I uncovered types of property that were not like the "private property" found in the West. Prominent among these were MegaChem (auto-cross-ownership) and Czech Press (simple self-ownership). In these property forms, some or all of the owners are essentially replaced by a managerial elite, close to what the Western managerialist theorists such as Berle and Means probably incorrectly thought was emerging in the United States (see Eyal, Szelenyi, and Townsley, 1998).

Still, in spite of all of these caveats, I think that the preponderance of evidence points to the emergence of capitalism in Eastern Europe. Hungary and the former Czechoslovakia have fundamentally been transformed into capitalist economies, in which control rights, and an increasing share of rights to income and to sell rest with nonstate actors. Already, the majority of firms are mostly "private" property—they are mostly market-dependent firms, hiring and firing free-wage labor as they accumulate and reinvest, moving from market to market (that is, line to line) to attempt to maximize their profits.

Thus, when I say that "capitalism has emerged" I mean that the most significant type of economic activity occurs between *market-dependent* units that are not *controlled* by the state. Much of this is owned (in the sense of having control rights, along with rights to residual income and the right to sell) by private individuals, although much is also owned by other firms, or other institutions. The statistical data that we have, almost all of it for Hungary, show that private property is indeed growing, and has done so at a fairly impressive pace. On the other hand, as of now, there is much less "capitalist ownership" than in other capitalist economies—there are more significant examples of "managerialism" and other ownership solutions, as Szelenyi and his collaborators have argued. What the future holds is beyond the realm of science, although we can make predictions and guesses. What we can be fairly sure of is that the future of private property is indeed growing, and has done so at a fairly impressive pace. The various strategies I identify in chapter 2 are descriptions of the ways in which these actors were able to "privatize" various property rights, wealth and networks of interrelated human capital and business contacts.

This finding of the existence of capitalist firms embedded in market structures, is supported by my qualitative fieldwork (which has been presented in the last five chapters) as well as by a good deal of statistical evidence (particularly for Hungary). In Hungary, by 1996, a full 76.5 percent of firms with more than 50 employees had at least 25 percent private ownership of one variety or the other, and state ownership of less than 25 percent. Another 5.5 percent of these firms have more than 25 percent private and state ownership, and these behave statistically much more like private firms than state firms. And only 1.7 percent of these "private" firms are owned by Hungarian banks, which are likely government-owned.

Thus, firms with over 50 employees in Hungary are dominated by private ownership. Firms of less than 50 employees constitute 99.4 percent of all firms in the economy (see Appendix 3), the vast majority of which are private. Even excluding the category of firms with ten or fewer employees (many of which are dummy firms), there are still four times as many firms with 11 to 50 employees as firms with more than 50 employees—and probably almost every one is private (although there are still a few small cooperatives around, and a few are possibly institutionally owned satellites in recombinant schemes).

One could argue against this finding, from Stark's theory of recombinant property, that even if there is formally private ownership and/or control in Hungary, there is still a great deal of blurring of firm boundaries. Stark would push my analysis and ask to what extent there is hedging activity by companies, a kind of system of reciprocity as opposed to market integration. Thus, Stark could argue that what is interesting is not necessarily the majority ownership and control of firms, but rather their ability to spread risk. Thus, what becomes interesting about the latest ownership data for Hungary is not the massive increase in the amount of private ownership per se, but the amount of ownership that is outside "private individual" ownership, and thus possibly constitutes "recombinant property." However, of the firms with 25 percent or more private ownership, only 9.5 percent of them have any state ownership, although 43.5 percent of them have some state, Hungarian firm or Hungarian bank ownership. This might well indicate that there is indeed some risk sharing going on. The lion's share, of course, is ownership by other Hungarian firms. Even if one half of these firms are really state owned (directly or through other state-owned firms), a very generous estimate, that still leaves more than 75 percent of the firms in the economy dominated by private owners.

Some of this interfirm ownership, no doubt, is recombinant property like Stark's example of Heavy Metal. Some involves cross-ownership strategies of creating capitalism without capitalists, and some is just horizontal and vertical integration, and does not differ from "private" property as found in the West. More empirical research is needed to try to understand the proportions of these different types of institutional ownership.

Of course, like all capitalist systems in the West and elsewhere, the postcommunist capitalist system is not purely capitalist. In fact it, more than other capitalist systems, retains much noncapitalist economic activity. Table 6.1 compares the characteristics of postcommunist and advanced Western capitalist systems.

In postcommunist central Europe, types of economic redistribution occur that are not very prevalent in the West. While the West probably has more welfare redistribution, postcommunist capitalism has much more subterranean redistribution by which the state bolsters firms. The same can be said for the clientelistic allocation of financial capital, which also exists in the West—witness the savings and loans scandal. The difference is that in the postcommunist capitalist economies, this seems the rule rather than the exception. There is also the existence of economic activity based on reciprocity, such as interenterprise debt creation (in essence, the firms gave themselves and their customers—firms that purchase their outputs—free credit). But recombinant property can also be conceptualized as reciprocity-dominated interfirm relations (combined with an element of parasitism). This is a property form which might characterize as much as 10 percent of the Hungarian economy, although we do not really have good measures of it. Table 6.2 details the various distribution of property rights in the different forms of property—the right to residual income, the right to control the production process, and the right to sell the property.

Table 6.1
A Comparison of Postcommunist and Advanced Western Capitalism

	Postcommunist capitalism	*Advanced Western capitalism*
Free markets	++++	++++
Welfare redistribution	++	+++
Subterranean redistribution	++++	++
Clientelistic finance	++++	+
Political capitalism	++++	++
Interfirm reciprocity	+++	+
Parasitic satellites	+++	+
Separation of transfer and control rights	++++	+

Table 6.2
Distribution of Property Rights by Strategy of Transition

Strategy	*Income*	*Control*	*Transfer*
Clone company	Domestic person	Domestic person	Domestic person
MBO	Managers	Managers	Managers
FDI	Foreign capital	Foreign capital	Foreign capital
JVs	Foreign & domestic	Foreign & domestic	Foreign & domestic
MEBOs	Managers & some employee	Managers & some employee	Managers & some employee
Employee Buy-outs	Managers & employees	Managers & employees	Managers & employees
Satellites	Managers	Managers	Managers
Simple self-ownership	Outsiders & managers	Managers	Outsiders & managers
Auto-cross-ownership	Managers	Managers	Managers
State-owned	State	State & managers	State
Leases	Managers & state	Managers	State

In postcommunist Hungary and the former Czechoslovakia, there was a much looser coupling of these property rights than in the typical picture of the West. There was especially more separation of ownership and control, in which managers seemed in some instances to have much control but no real rights to sell the property. The state also frequently has some formal ownership, and thus rights to residual income and to sell, much more than in most Western economies. (Although the amount of state ownership in Austria, the Western country with the highest amount of state ownership, probably exceeds the figure for Hungary.)

DEVELOPMENTAL CONSEQUENCES

How does one speculate on the developmental consequences of various types of property? Social scientists are only mildly successful at postdicting the past, and their record for predicting the future is even weaker. On top of this, we must recognize that the theory of "economic development"—the theory of what types of property lead to quantitative and qualitative growth—is fairly weak, fragmented, and hotly contested. Perhaps the safest way to proceed would be simply to specify the division of property rights resulting from the different "strategies of transition," and to evaluate the expected effects from different theoretical perspectives.

With the property rights specified for each form, it now becomes possible to speculate on their developmental consequences.

The emerging neoclassical/neo-Marxist orthodoxy on this point is that "capitalist" property relations—as found in private ownership either foreign or domestic—are the most "dynamic" in terms of developing the productive forces and the economy. These relations are responsible for rising labor productivity and rising living standards. This reasoning has strong support among the classics, as Smith, Marx and Weber all had reasons to believe that capitalism would lead to the dynamic expansion of the economy. And indeed, the historical record demonstrates that capitalist economies—more specifically mixed social formations with a dominant logic of economic activity based on capitalist accumulation—have produced more quantitative and qualitative growth over the long run than other attempted ways of organizing economic life. Of course, the neo-Marxists would argue that while capitalism is more efficient economically than "actually existing" socialism or "bureaucratic state-socialism," "true socialism" in which the planning process is democratized is bound to be more economically efficient yet.

Brenner's neo-Marxist formulation is an exceptionally clear example of this reasoning. Brenner argues that capitalist social property relations lead to a systematic plowing of surplus back into the productive process through specialization and innovation, leading to rising labor productivity. In Brenner's schema, capitalism is defined as having three components: (1) private property, (2) free wage labor, and (3) generalized commodity production. Private property and a domination of markets means there are economic actors with relatively hard budget constraints (the actors are market-dependent)—faced with competition but unable to respond by systematically increasing the absolute rate of surplus appropriation.

In other words, private capitalists have to maximize profits in the face of competition to stay alive, but are unable to squeeze labor by increasing the intensity of labor or the length of labor time per unit of pay, because "free wage laborers" can take employment with another capitalist. Thus, capitalists will systematically accumulate, specialize and innovate. In noncapitalist systems, this pressure to accumulate, specialize and innovate in order to maximize the price: cost ratio is not necessarily present. In precapitalist systems, the directly producing class, such as peasants, may well not be separated from the means of subsistence and means of production. Peasants don't specialize, accumulate and innovate because they pursue a "safety-first" strategy and like to subdivide their holdings (Brenner 1976). Under "state-socialism" Brenner would argue that (1) workers are not really separated from the means of production, and (2) there is no market-dependence because of the pervasiveness of soft-budget constraints. The first condition would mean that production cannot move lines easily, and labor cannot be disciplined as efficiently. The lack of market-dependence would mean that there was no systematic pressure forcing increases in labor productivity—rather, a "political logic" would probably develop.

There is a lot to recommend the emerging orthodoxy—perhaps it is justified, as a "tightening" of paradigms can be a good thing at times. However, I do not want to engage in this debate at this time, as I do not have anything to add to it. I call this view a new emerging "orthodoxy" because neoclassical economists and neo-Institutionalist economists, in addition to many neo-Marxists and Marxists, would agree with this reasoning.

From this perspective, the clone companies, MBOs, JVs, FDI and MEBOs would be the most "promising" property forms. That is because they are most like the forms in the West. Employee buy-outs would also probably be positively regarded, as at least they eliminate agent-principal problems and create private property. Of course, this form is less "desirable" than the others because theorists suspect (and probably correctly) that employees will not fire themselves frequently enough, nor will they want to relocate production or move line to line.

Continued state ownership would of course be an anathema—so the more privatization the better. Satellites are clearly wasteful. These types of firms will have an essentially negative economic effect. No incentive exists to promote reinvesting the financial resources "extracted" from the mother company in any productive activity, although this may well happen if it is invested in a new (real) private company. Long-term parasitic satellites have a particularly deleterious effect, as they deny the parent company the funds needed to carry out necessary economic restructuring. Also, the primary activity of many of these companies is purely commercial, adding one extra, unnecessary, and inefficient step in the commodity chain—this is "rent-seeking" behavior.

Creating a clone of a division is a strategy that hurts state enterprises because much of their "variable capital" disappears, and the resources used to build the "human capital" of its employees is lost. To the neoclassical economist, this would be good, as it would "hasten the decline" of these "socialist dinosaurs." Believers in the new orthodoxy would point out that these firms were often too big and inefficient from the diseconomies of scale and overbureaucratization inherited from Communist overindustrialization. Thus, these clones create competitors in an otherwise very monopolized economy. They are truly capitalist (early capitalist actually, in terms of their property rights and control relations), and have the incentive structure and the ability to monitor their firms which should channel profits into productive reinvestment. Furthermore, when these firms bring in foreign capital by forming small partnerships they secure foreign direct investment.

Of course, to the neoclassical economist, foreign direct investment can provide capital for investment in capital-starved economies, provide jobs, stimulate aggregate demand, provide access to Western markets that might be protected (as well as marketing support in those markets), and provide competition in a previously highly monopolized industrial structure. The adoption of strategies of joining forces with foreign capitalists can only be a good thing from this perspective.

MEBOs and simple self-ownership strategies, from this paradigm, would be seen as likely to lead to economic development. MEBOs, which comprise a significant portion of the postcommunist economy, as argued in chapter 4, create a bundle of property rights which are capitalistic as well as efficient, according to most observers. This is largely a result of the elimination of principal-agent dilemmas that occur with insider ownership. Managers who pursue MEBO strategies are probably not pilfering funds through satellites. If they were, they would not bother to use capital to gain ownership rights over their firm (pirates do not usually bother themselves with the long-term integrity of the ships they are raiding). Also, by helping managers secure control of their firms, they make it more likely that the firm will have a coherent long-term business strategy, which is of great importance in the postcommunist context, in which disinterested absentee ownership is so prevalent (and harmful for the firm). Firms that result from a strategy of simple self-ownership should have all the advantages, and types of behavior, as the MEBOs.

The neoclassical economists would have a completely different take on the strategy of auto-cross-ownership, such as MegaChem. On the one hand, MegaChem is taking property outside of the government's direct ownership, and thus it is good. Furthermore, such firms should have the principal-agent advantages that management buy-outs theoretically enjoy. On the other hand, such analysts might depict MegaChem as a monopolist that serves to artificially keep out foreign products and is thus practicing *de facto* protectionism. Furthermore, they might argue that cross-enterprise ownership simply softens budget constraints, and is thereby likely to lead to inefficient firms by preventing firms from being liquidated.

Other theoretical traditions/paradigms would view the developmental consequences of the different strategies somewhat differently. In particular, analysts starting from a dependency/world systems perspective would evaluate the developmental potential of various property forms rather differently than would the neo-orthodox. A particular source of disagreement, obviously, would be in the interpretation of the role of foreign capital.

Chapter 3 detailed different types of foreign investment that result from adopting a strategy of creating a partnership with foreign capital. A dependency theorist would no doubt be attracted to the likelihood that some of this behavior might fairly be described as *comprador*, in particular when multinationals purchase an entire market and extract monopoly rents after eliminating domestic producers. In the worst case scenario, these firms would then repatriate most of their profits without reinvesting any in the country. Dependency and world systems theorists argue this would lead to the "development of underdevelopment" or the "peripheralization" of non-Western economies.

Observers shaped by this perspective would have a different view of auto-cross-ownership than the neoclassical thinkers. Dependency/world system theorists would argue that companies like MegaChem allow the concentration of capital on a national basis, as opposed to allowing foreign capital to dominate industry. This is beneficial for long-term economic development because it cuts down on parasitic and surplus-draining behavior (such as repatriating profit or replacing local products with imports).

This type of "exotic" ownership, dependency theorists could argue, also allows for the combination of assets which make it more likely the firm can operate on the economies of scale necessary to compete on most world markets. The amalgamation of companies into these groups probably creates enterprises large enough to hope to compete with the massive multinational corporations that might otherwise dominate the Czech economy and the world market. For example, MegaChem competes directly with Chevron as one of the world's two producers of Alfaolifines, for which there is a huge new market. From a world systems perspective, spawning multinational companies to exploit other economies may be the best way to move towards the "core," as South Korea has done (10 of the largest 500 multinationals are now Korean).

Furthermore, they would point out that a larger proportion of the profits from foreign multinationals are likely to find their way outside of Eastern Europe as compared to a domestically based firm. This is probably true except in places where political capitalism is dominant, as in Russia, where the domestic ownership class exports significant profits and assets to the West. For example, all profits from MegaChem were reinvested in modernizing their member companies.

Dependency theorists could also rebut the neoclassical criticism that in a firm like MegaChem budget constraints will be soft. They would argue that budget constraints are still borne by the holding company, creating the incentive for the jettisoning (or massive restructuring) of poorly performing firms within the group. Furthermore, this cross-ownership and "regulated competition" allows for the reinvestment of profits in production. This is extremely important because of the obsolete nature of much of the capital stock of many postcommunist firms. The reinvestment of profits is facilitated by managerial control because, in the absence of any real principal separate from the agent, there is almost no incentive for diverting profits into dividends. Thus, MegaChem allowed its troubled subsidiaries to keep all their profits for reinvestment in productive equipment (which is quite massive and expensive in this sector), and decided to give no dividends for the next few years while they strengthen the capital stock of the group. Furthermore, the existence of financial organizations in the groups (as in the Japanese *keretsu*) allows for firms to attain credit for needed expansion.

Perhaps a third way to think about development might consist of "sociological neo-Institutionalists"—to be distinguished from "economic neo-Institutionalists. These researchers would stress that "organizational diversity" is likely to lead to adaptability. According to this perspective, the more types of economic organizations that exist, the more adaptable the overall economy will be in the long run (see Stark 1989). Thus, even if all forms are not maximally efficient at any given time, over the long run, because of the existence of economic crises and continual change, the economy with more organizational diversity would have an advantage. In other words, they do not want to put all their "property eggs" in one basket. Such economists would welcome the diversity of property forms, although they would certainly condemn the parasitic behavior of satellites.

In addition to the different types of firms resulting from the different transition strategies, one must consider the effects of other types of "nonmarket" integration that I have identified. How do we evaluate those firms whose boundaries are blurred with the state (if they partake of subterranean redistribution), with political institutions (if they practice political-capitalist strategies), and with clientelist relationships with sources of investment capital (as exists with the use of the clientelistic access to finance)?

Subterranean redistribution, from the sociological-institutionalist and the dependency perspective, has had the positive economic effect of preventing massive bankruptcies which might have totally and irreparably destroyed the capitalist economies of postcommunist East Central Europe. The neo-orthodox would counter that subterranean redistribution weakens a firm's hard-budget constraints. Of course, in reality these constraints are still pretty hard in most cases, because there can be no guarantee for the firm that this type of "redistribution" will be forthcoming in the future. More research on the permanence of these structures is needed.

Clientelistic access to capital must be seen as far more deleterious from all perspectives. As Schumpter emphasized, the essence of a capitalist system is based on entrepreneurial activity utilizing borrowed money. The neo-orthodox would emphasize that credit provides a big part of the dynamism of capitalist society because it enables firms to switch lines of production or change the production process quickly. In Central Eastern Europe, the effects of these clientelistic networks are to (1) channel funds toward firms in clientelistic networks, and (2) raise the cost of capital, starving efficient firms without the correct network ties of capital to invest. This is bad for the long-term and even medium-term growth of the economy. This view is consonant with dependency theory as well as sociological new-institutionalism.

Like the effects of clientelism, political capitalism, most agree, is quite deleterious from a developmental viewpoint. Weber succinctly wrote of political capitalism: "It is clear from the very beginning that the politically-oriented events and processes which open up these profit opportunities exploited by political capitalism are irrational from an economic point of view—that is, from the point of view of orientation to market advantages and thus to the consumption needs of budgetary units" (Weber 1978: 116).

The neo-orthodox would argue that political-capitalist strategies create firms and allow them to stay in business through noneconomic processes, and therefore these firms are probably less efficient than ones that are purely market-dependent. Firms reliant on political connections will have an incentive to put some of their resources into maintaining those political connections. And, like political accumulation under feudalism (see Brenner 1986), maintaining "political communities" means spending money on political lobbying and the conspicuous consumption of luxury goods. Furthermore, both the neo-orthodox and the sociological institutionalists would agree that when property rights are allocated on the basis of personal networks with the incumbents in positions of political authority, the security of property rights are undermined, thereby creating an incentive not to invest resources in the newly acquired company for fear that ownership might be changed once again—an extension of what Mertlik (1996) aptly calls "pre-privatization agony."

EMPIRICAL EVIDENCE ON THE ECONOMIC EFFECTS OF OWNERSHIP

Aside from the unproven speculation and prediction on this point, there is some empirical evidence concerning the performance of different types of property. For example, with regards to perhaps the greatest controversy, the role of foreign capital, I have some direct experience. In my interviews, five firms were 50 percent to 100 percent owned by foreign capital. Of these, none fell in the category of "predatory" investors as described by dependency theorists. On the contrary, these firms were obviously an asset to the Czech, Slovakian and Hungarian economies respectively. In some of them, however, there was a tendency to move toward low-tech production techniques.

The property rights were clear in these firms, and ownership and control were aligned so that no satellite firms were possible. They were almost certainly among the most efficient firms in the postcommunist economies. Other research has borne this out as well (Hamar 1994: 186–190; Dobosiewicz 1992: 28).

This was also corroborated by one author's examination of Hungarian state-generated statistics:

One of the more surprising facts to arise out of this review of Hungarian State statistics for 1990 is the relatively high level of profitability among joint ventures in Hungary. Given that most joint ventures are "new" companies, with high initial start up costs, it would be expected that the majority would make losses in the first few years. This is not the case in Hungary, where, in 1990, 56 percent of companies with foreign participation recorded a profit. In fact the total profits of joint ventures doubled between 1989 and 1990—to Ft49.6 billion ($785 million)—although it should be noted that the number of joint ventures increased by about five times. Losses increased even more rapidly, but the net effect was a 68 percent increase in overall profits to Ft37 billion ($585 million). (Young 1993: 117)

Furthermore, according to Young, in 1990 joint ventures paid Ft12.4 billion ($200 million) in dividends—fully 44 percent of all dividends by Hungarian companies. Of this, Ft4.2 billion ($65 million) were able to be repatriated. But, according to the national bank of Hungary, only Ft2.3 billion was actually repatriated—so that about five sixths of the profit was either saved domestically or reinvested in Hungary. Young also claims that while most companies laid off people, JVs doubled their number of employees in 1991 to 4.5 percent of the workforce, even though their productivity was twice as high as other types of firms (which should have decreased the need for adding labor), and their wages were 35 percent higher for white collar and 11 percent higher for blue-collar workers. (1993: 118–119). Finally, advocates would point out, foreign firms have imported much capital, making it easier for Hungary to service its foreign debt (Hamar 1994: 187).

STATISTICAL EVIDENCE OF FIRM PERFORMANCE

We have some quantitative data that are of some relevance in these regards. The 1996 Tarki data set, 293 randomly sampled firms from among the Hungarian population of firms with over 50 employees, allows us to develop some rough ideas about the economic performance of firms with various types of ownership (Table 6.3).

What do these data tell us about the economic performance of firms with different types of ownership? First, we see that firms without a strong owner, or with fragmented ownership (no category of owner has 25 percent or more ownership), are less profitable, and are less likely to have invested at least 10 million forints and employed new labor in 1996. The other interesting finding is that foreign firms seem to be adding more to the economy than other types of firms. Foreign firms disproportionately invest more than 10 million forints and disproportionately employ

Table 6.3
Profits, Expansion and Reinvestment by Type of Owner in 1996

Groups owning more than 25%	Number of firms	Were profitable	Invested over 10 million HUF	Employed new labor
No strong Owner	14	42.9%	28.6%	14.3%
State	39	61.5%	46.2%	23.1%
Private domestic (including MBOs)	136	69.1%	46.0%	27.0%
Foreign	60	54.8%	75.8%	42.6%
Employee (not MBOs)	20	80.0%	40.0%	15.0%
State & private	16	75.0%	50.0%	37.5%

new labor (thereby creating jobs). Furthermore, foreign ownership is less profitable than either state, private, or employee ownership. This might be due to foreign firms having less access to political sources of profit, or it might be due to the extensive use of satellite strategies in conjunction with domestic ownership strategies, as discussed in chapter 4. These firms, typically a manager and employee buy-out (MEBO), might be extra profitable because the use of satellite strategies during their establishment enabled the buyers to privatize only profitable assets. This would probably elevate the profitability of firms in the "private" category, because the category includes management buy-outs—which were quite profitable in the 1992 Tarki data set, and judging by the 80 percent profitability rate among employee-owned firms in the 1996 data, are also likely to have remained quite profitable.

So what can we conclude, overall, about the role of foreign direct investment in the transition to capitalism in postcommunist East Central Europe? First, we have reason to believe that, if not for foreign direct investment, the postcommunist credit crunch would have been even worse, especially in Hungary. Second, foreign direct investment brings tight ownership and control regardless of which form it takes, because it rests on a mutuality of interests of former socialist managers and foreign partners. Creating tight ownership and control in firms is quite important in the postcommunist context, because many types of parasitic managerial strategies are possible when ownership and control are radically separated.

Integration with foreign capital (not necessarily foreign direct investment) seems a necessary, if not a sufficient, means of "catching up" with the West. Our focus should center on the various ways in which foreign contact is mediated, and consider the different types of investment. Such analysis could potentially inform postcommunist economic policy.

Integration that is based on purchasing formerly domestic distribution channels, and doing low-value-added contract work, is not likely to close the gap
between Eastern and Western Europe. What is needed is foreign investment in
highly skilled manufacturing enterprises that export to Western Europe. Such
investment is likely to combine recently obsolete technology from the West (or the
Far East, in particular South Korea) with much cheaper, but still highly skilled,
labor, which when combined with the low transportation costs to Western Europe,
can be quite profitable in the long run.

These findings supporting the developmental virtues of foreign investment,
while seemingly strong, appear to be slightly at odds with these other statistical
indicators.

The data in Table 6.4 are striking for the fact that foreign ownership has much
less growth in fixed capital and less growth in turnover than the other types of
ownership, in spite of greater investment and greater expansion of employment.
What this might mean is that foreign firms are investing heavily in variable capital. This expansion could either be in training people or expansion by adding low-
wage production (I saw examples of both in my fieldwork). Also interesting is the
relatively lower levels of increases in fixed capital by private firms—perhaps a
result of a relative lack of access to subterranean redistribution or clientelistic
access to financial resources. Or, since state-owned firms have the lowest debt,
they may have more money to invest in fixed capital (state firms had the lowest
rate of indebtedness,[1] perhaps the result of much bad debt being shifted to the
government during their debt consolidation program— a major act of subterranean redistribution). Finally, it seems that state-owned firms have replaced
some of their very old capital, by putting in labor-saving machines which account
for their increase in fixed capital and low rate of turnover growth, but also high
rates of laying off workers (35.9 percent compared to 20.6 percent of private, 20
percent of foreign, 20 percent of employee, and 18.8 percent of mixed private/
state ownership).

Table 6.4
Fixed-Capital and Turnover Growth by Type of Ownership in 1996

Property types (at least 25% ownership)	Growth in fixed capital	Growth in turnover
No strong owner	21.4%	50.0%
State	38.5%	17.0%
Private (including MBOs)	20.0%	42.2%
Foreign	8.0%	22.6%
Employee	30.0%	50.0%
State & Private	37.6%	31.3%

EXPLAINING DIFFERENCES IN TYPES OF FIRMS IN DIFFERENT POSTCOMMUNIST COUNTRIES

While I argue that Hungary, the Czech Republic and Slovakia, and also, I believe, East Germany, Poland and Slovenia, can be understood by the model of post-communist capitalism I have elaborated in this book, there are, nonetheless, very real differences between the various postcommunist countries.

For example, Table 6.5 shows that Hungarian firms are smaller than firms in the Czech Republic.

In interpreting these results we should remember that the Czech and Hungarian samples are not identical. The Czech firms are taken from the largest 3000 industrial firms, while the Hungarian firms are sampled from the largest 3000 firms overall, including nonindustrials.

Hungary's smaller firms are desirable from any theoretical vantage point because they increase the probability of a tighter identity of ownership and control. This makes parasitic behavior by managers less likely. They are problematic, especially in the world system/dependency view, because it is harder to capture economies of scale. However, in general, even among the bigger firms I studied in Hungary, a tendency toward a tighter relationship between ownership and control was evident. This was partially the result of the mass voucher privatization scheme in the Czech Republic, which created very dispersed ownership patterns resulting from investment fund owners with very low monitoring capacity.

Hungary also has much greater foreign participation in the economy than does the Czech Republic (17.6 percent of the largest industrial firms were majority owned by foreigners in 1992 in Hungary, versus just 5.6 percent in the Czech Republic). Finally, a major difference between the types of firms in the Czech Republic and Hungary is found in auto-cross-ownership, such as in the Czech Business Groups. The evaluation of these facts would, again, diverge between the neoclassical/neo-Marxist and the dependency/world system views.

Table 6.5
Firm Size as Measured by Employees in Czech and Hungarian Industry in 1993

Number of employees	Czech industry (N = 257)	Hungarian industry (N = 404)
1–24	0.0%	13.4%
25–99	39.0%	29.0%
100–499	43.0%	39.6%
500–1999	14.0%	13.6%
2000 and above	4.0%	2.6%

Source: Hungarian data is based on the 1992 Tarki data, and Czech data on a mail survey of 257 firms (returned from a questionnaire sent to a random sample of 1000 of the 3000 largest industrial firms) in the Czech Republic (Zemplinerova, Lastovicka and Marcincin 1995).

HOW, THEN, DO WE EXPLAIN THESE DIFFERENCES?

To understand differences among the various countries, I think it is necessary to add a historical dimension—to explore the country-specific institutional legacies of late communism. Because these societies were primarily driven by a political logic, their institutional differences are the result of differences in the political systems. I find an analysis of legitimacy useful for these purposes. Following Weber (1978), legitimacy is seen as involving the maintenance of a stable arrangement for "sharing" power and other resources (the means of administration) between the king and his henchmen, the executive and his staff. Or, to put it in a slightly different way, between various groups within the "elite." In addition, Weber saw that system legitimacy was also dependent on the "masses" (understood as all nonelite groups) accepting the right of the elite to rule (whether out of habit, belief in a set of legal-rational principles, or a belief in the personal greatness of a charismatic leader).

During the Communist period in the Czech Republic and Hungary, legitimacy struggles and solutions decisively shaped the organization of the economy. The resulting differences in industrial organization in the two countries had a profound effect in structuring the postcommunist firms after the fall of the Communist Party.

As the path-dependency approach suggests (Stark 1992), the postcommunist order does not develop in a vacuum, but as the result of strategies that were formulated in an institutional environment evolving out of the old Communist systems. This is not to imply a simple structural determination of postcommunist development from Communist-created structures. The future of postcommunism significantly depends upon the activities of various people. Among these activities are decisions about institutional innovation and transformation made by the economic and political elites, and, when mobilized, other social groups. Therefore, although there is a structural background that significantly influences the outcome of historical development, this outcome is in no way simply "determined" by these structures. Numerous contingencies are causally implicated, including the "contingent" selection of some strategies and the rejection of others by various actors (see Sahlins 1991; Sewell Jr. 1992a and 1992b on contingency).

I find with Stark that "institutional continuity" is furthered by the persistence of networks formed between the incumbents of various organizations that may no longer exist. These social networks are extremely important resources to be mobilized by actors to attain their goals in the emergent systems (as they are in the advanced capitalist "nontransitional" economies as well) (see Granoveter 1985).

In Hungary, Communism had always been much "weaker" (as it had a more fragile legitimacy) than in the Czech Republic, largely because of the development of the prewar class structure and the overlap of an identification of "Communism" with nationalism in the latter country. Communist legitimacy was also weakened in Hungary by the terror created by the Communist government following the First World War. In addition, the Czechoslovakian Communist elite experienced a more severe repression than their Hungarian counterparts from the late 1960s on. This created a structure of legitimacy that, from the late 1960s, relied on recentralizing control within the elite. By contrast, in Hungary the Communist Party sought to maintain its legitimacy by decentralizing control within the elite.

Legitimacy and economic control are related by the fact that the "decentralization" of decision-making power creates more autonomy for the activities of managers and technical experts and shields them from the interference of members of the bureaucratic estate. Thus, in Hungary, elite legitimacy was structured by a greater toleration of freedom, as well as an increase in power at the firm-management level to organize production. Mass legitimacy was "secured" by a constantly rising standard of living for the majority of the population. This was probably the result of the 1956 revolution, during which Communists were strung up on lamp poles and external military intervention was required to restore them to power. Prior to the revolution, the Hungarian economy had hit a classic crisis of the "shortage economy," arising from the noncoordinated activity of various economic actors. Thus, many of the Communist elite interpreted these events as the result of economic stagnation, with resultant decreases in the living standards of the Hungarian population.

This had several consequences. In the Hungarian economy, as compared to the Czech economy, there was more "decentralization," probably resulting in the increased dispersal of social networks among firm-level actors, and leading to the breakup of state enterprises into smaller firms than those that existed in the Czech Republic. Hungary, in an effort to reap economic benefits from participation in the world economy, was more open to foreign participation than was the Czech Republic. This created network ties between foreign firms and Hungarian managers that were mobilized to create new joint-venture firms, or to privatize divisions of state enterprises in Hungary much more frequently than in the Czech Republic.

The Hungarian elite, unlike their Czech counterparts, also borrowed enormous amounts of money in the late Communist period to increase consumption for legitimacy purposes. Most of this money was used for internal consumption, especially for the personal construction of homes. This resulted in a state desperate to pay off its debt, and a system where credit for firms to innovate and make investments has become extremely expensive (twice as high as in the Czech Republic), because the government crowds out borrowing and drives up interest rates. It also creates a state particularly intent on selling off valuable assets to foreign companies in an attempt to escape their fiscal crisis. This probably explains why Hungary has privatized even natural monopolies (as with the recent privatization of the Hungarian electrical power distribution sector).

Finally, it seems that the Czech Republic has a novel form of auto-cross-ownership within a vertically and horizontally integrated group of enterprises. Networks mobilized to create this organizational form were probably formed at the ministerial level, in particular within the branch of the Ministry of Industry, which coordinated this entire sector. This "coordination," of course, consisted of actors from the government, banks and the firms participating in "plan-bargaining" during the Communist period. Perhaps MegaChem is an example of this—the president and CEO of the whole group had been made a member of the Politburo two months before the Communist Party collapsed.

NOTE

1. According to the 1996 data set 64.1% of state-owned firms have no debt compared to 44.9% of privately-owned firms, 44.1% of employee-owned firms, and 43.8% of state and private mixes.

Appendix 1

Quantitative Data

There are two original data sets upon which I rely for the statistical analysis of the structure and transformation of the postcommunist firm. The first was the most detailed firm-level questionnaire fielded on the postcommunist firm, written by myself, Akos Rona-Tas, and Ivan Szelenyi as a mail-survey supplement to the 1993 Treiman and Szelenyi Elite Survey, which did not ask questions directly about the characteristics of the firm, but rather about the CEO who ran the firm. This instrument was rather long (six pages), and was mailed to 600 randomly sampled firms from a list of the largest 3000 firms in 1993. This larger list was taken from the *Hoppenstadt*, a German Eastern European business directory compiled for most of the countries in Eastern Europe. By the time the mail survey was sent out in 1995, 150 firms no longer existed, and of the remaining 450 firms, 83 sent back completed questionnaires. The other firms were contacted by phone, where a shorter version of the questionnaire was administered. An additional 61 surveys were completed in this fashion, bringing the total number of surveys up to 144 for an overall response rate of 32 percent.

This questionnaire would have provided the best data yet on the structure of the postcommunist firm if it had had a larger sample size or response rate. Nonetheless, the number of firms still allows for tests of significance. Indeed, the small number of firms means that any statistically significant finding will have to be quite strong not to be considered the result of chance.

This data set allows me to test specific details about ownership and interfirm relationships, since the questions were designed to explore just that variable. In particular, I wrote questions to allow me to get at the industrial organization of the firm—that is, information about interrelationships between buyers and sellers. This is particularly important for testing David Stark's theory of recombinant property. In addition, I was able to ask questions about firms' relationships to banks, their investment policies and so forth.

This data set was essentially duplicated by Hungarian researchers that used the firm TARKI to conduct a 1996 interview-based survey. The resulting data, because they used the much more expensive method of interviews, are far superior—the number of responses is 293, a marked improvement over the mail survey.

The third data set, compiled by the Hungarian research institute TARKI, will be used to create a rough breakdown of the different types of property in the Hungarian economy in 1992, and to provide a point of comparison for use with the 1996 survey, so that the change in property forms over the last four years is discernible. It is the biggest firm-level questionnaire ever conducted on a random sample of firms in Hungary that takes into account detailed ownership information.

This survey, based on the Szelenyi-Treiman survey, asked direct questions about the firm, and thereby greatly enhanced its value for this book. The survey was paid for by Hungarian banks, and contained additional marketing research information about the firms' banking preferences. There were 1001 randomly sampled firms from the largest 3000 firms in 1992, as listed in the *Hoppenstadt*. The CEOs or other top management members were interviewed by the Tarki field workers, who persisted until all 1001 firms were interviewed. Because of its very large size, if slightly less-detailed questions, statistics generated by this survey will be of particular importance for this book.

Appendix 2

Qualitative Methodology

These case studies are primarily the result of interviews I conducted with firm-level actors—CEOs, owners, or other major management figures. Basically, I wanted to interview the people best qualified to speak about the history of the firms—the strategic considerations, the external environment and the internal relationships. This person was, naturally, the executive with the most authority—very often the firm's founder and owner. Thus, my approach was to study many firms in an attempt to capture the diversity of the various organizational forms other writers had led me to expect to find.

In all, I conducted interviews at about 50 firms in four countries. The lion's share of the interviews were conducted in Hungary and the Czech Republic, but some were conducted in Slovakia and another handful in Slovenia as well. Consequently, and not at all surprisingly, I produce a more complex picture of property changes and property structures than the theorists considered.

In conducting these case studies, I followed the advice of Robert Park and the Chicago school: I went out and got the seat of my pants dirty. There is no established method for doing this kind of research—I basically went to Eastern Europe and improvised. I spent the fall of 1995 in Hungary and the Czech Republic conducting my research. From January to June of 1996 I was fortunate to be awarded a fellowship at the Institute fur die Wissenschaften vom Menschen in Vienna—an institute designed to bring together scholars from the West and East. Because of the institute's location in Vienna, I was able to use it as a base to conduct additional interviews in Hungary, the Czech Republic, Slovakia and Slovenia. The location, one hour from Bratislava, three hours from Budapest and six hours from Prague and Ljubliana, was ideal for this purpose. I took many extended trips from Vienna,which lasted anywhere from a night to a week.

My case studies were selected to represent a wide variety of firms, including foreign-owned, domestic-owned and state-owned, in various lines of production and of various sizes. In addition, I also conducted interviews wherever I could. Whenever possible, firms were matched for product line in the different countries.

The most challenging part of this research consisted of actually obtaining appointments to conduct the interviews. This was difficult because CEOs are busy people, and in Eastern Europe many had already been inundated with Westerners looking for privatization bargains. The problem, sociologically speaking, was how to gain access to elites, who, following C. Wright Mills (1956), are people with power and authority by virtue of their position in organizations.

I ended up employing several means to obtain interviews. My first strategy was to employ one or more bilingual research assistants—either college students or graduate students—to contact firms from a list I compiled. They were instructed to explain my project and set up interviews. I had them explain the purpose of the interview, and assure potential interviewees it would be anonymous and would last less than an hour. In practice, most interviews lasted from one to three hours, with some lasting an entire evening over food and wine.

I also typically took a tour of any production facilities (often I conducted the interviews at the corporate headquarters). Although most of my interviewees spoke English (since this is indeed the international business language[1]) in some cases I used translators. I never recorded the interviews, assuming that this would inhibit the interviewees, especially because I was interested in some illegal behavior. I simply took notes in shorthand, and typed them into my computer as soon as possible.

My success in this strategy depended on the persistence and talent of the particular research assistants I employed (which in part depended on my compensation scheme). The most effective strategy was to follow up a fax with a phone call.

My first strategy for selecting firms was to use a list drawn up from various business registers. A second strategy I employed was to ask local academic elites in Eastern Europe for contacts—the names of managers I could interview. Here my tenure at the institute in Vienna was invaluable, as it was the ideal place to make contacts with such elites. Most helpful in this regard was Ivan Szelenyi, who sent letters of introduction to many firms in Hungary for me. A third strategy I employed was to draw on my family's resources—a family friend is a multimillion-dollar importer of chemicals from the Czech Republic, and he helped me gain access to several major firms. Finally, when I conducted an interview, I was able to ask for the name of someone else I could interview.

I was somewhat surprised and greatly relieved to obtain interviews with CEOs and other top managers from approximately 45 firms in Hungary, Slovakia and the Czech Republic, and I obtained another five in Slovenia. Appendix 1 describes these firms.

The CEOs that agreed to be interviewed did so for a variety of reasons. First, whenever I had a letter of introduction, or the name of an associate who referred me, things went smoothly. These interviewees agreed to see me out of respect for the referring person. For example, I interviewed one of five members of the Board of Directors of an enormous Czech conglomerate (he was also the CEO of five of the 60 companies in this group). After thanking him for taking the time to see me, he informed me that he had no choice as one of his business associates had requested it.

Others, at less prestigious or powerful firms, thought that they might have something to gain by meeting me. Interestingly, my presence as a researcher from America was, on more than one occasion, perceived as potentially an opportunity— somehow or someway—to make a business contact. Indeed, at the very first firm I visited, the manager of a large clothing manufacturer in Western Hungary wanted to find a buyer for off-season production. Even after the interview was completed, he didn't quite believe that I was an academic interested only in studying the transition. Still others met me because I was an American from a famous university. They figured that if I came all the way from America—and from California, no less—they could take the time to meet me.

Once they agreed to meet me, of course, there was still the question of whether they would talk openly. Once again, to my surprise and relief, most were quite forthcoming. The few who were not I did not include in my sample of case studies. It seems that I was deemed safe to speak with because I was a foreigner, not a member of the press, and because the interviews were anonymous. Also I think that many of the interviewees, once they agreed to meet with me, felt a need to make my trip worthwhile. Many were quite happy, and even seemed relieved, to tell me about the transition process. Their lives had been consumed by the process of their firm's transformation, and the interview gave them the opportunity to reflect on this process and put it in perspective for themselves as well as for me. Indeed, I got the impression that some interviewees were desperate to tell their story once they had an excuse to do so.

In one particularly poignant example, I met with the CEO of a large, famous Czech trading company. I entered an impressive-looking building which was literally empty except for the new CEO. The interviewee, my translator and I, entered a lavish corporate meeting room with an enormous table and began the interview. At first the interview did not produce anything of special interest—just run-of-the-mill answers that pretended everything was fine when, clearly, everything was not fine: I continued to ask about the problems of the firm. Finally, the interviewee went to his office and emerged with a bottle of imported scotch. He offered me some, and I declined. When he offered a second time I accepted. He then poured all three of us quite generous drinks, downed his in one gulp, momentarily rolled his eyes back in his head, and proceeded to detail what had happened to his firm. This firm had been vitiated by the parasitic behavior of the former managers, and he had been brought in to try to clean up the mess. Furthermore, he detailed his firm's relationship to its primary bank, a story which invoked images of debt bondage. Two hours later, when he was finished, he insisted that this be kept confidential, but he looked quite relieved. He asked for a copy of whatever paper I ended up writing with this information.

As I did more and more interviews, I became skilled in asking questions and getting answers. I discovered that the interviews went better when I began by assuring the interviewees that I empathized with their difficult situations. I empathized with these interviewees, with their problems and the challenges of trying to do their jobs in the enormously uncertain economic environment of post-communism. I developed a sense of knowing whether or not someone was hiding something. I became accustomed to reading between the lines. Frequently I would ask questions more than once, framing them in a different way. Usually, after an hour or so, once I had gained the trust of the interviewees, they would answer questions they refused to answer earlier in the interview.

They also answered questions because they knew that there were some publicly available data with which I could corroborate their responses. In Hungary this was especially true, since the Court of Firm Registry requires extremely detailed information for every firm. This resource was used to corroborate my interviews, and I found no disagreements.

NOTE

1. Thus, a Polish and a Hungarian businessman would typically talk to each other in English, not Russian or even German.

Appendix 3

Description of Case Studies

HUNGARY

	Activity	Number of Employees
Case 1	Textile factory	1800
Case 2	Branch of a European commercial bank	30
Case 3	Electronic equipment maker, installer and servicer	40
Case 4	Electronic machinery manufacturer, importer, distributor and servicer	25
Case 5	Chemical firm	250
Case 6	Hospital equipment importer, distributor, installer and servicer	15
Case 7	Agribusiness	300
Case 8	Financial consultants	7
Case 9	Wood furniture producer	300
Case 10	Regional electricity distributor	400
Case 11	Diversified holding company	2500 (Many more, including employees of firms they partially own)
Case 12	Agrarian trading company (group)	1300

Case 13 Chemical-industry machine maker	160
Case 14 Petroleum industry planning and machines	500
Case 15 Petroleum producer and processor	19000
Case 16 Chemical industry	3000
Case 17 Telecommunications components	800
Case 18 Chemical engineering	200
Case 19 Electronics manufacturer	1500

Compare the size of 1001 randomly sampled firms out of the 3000 largest in Hungary in 1993 to my sample:

Employees	*Top 3000*	*My Sample (N = 19)*
Less than 25	22.8%	10.5%
25–99	28.4%	15.8%
100–299	23.4%	15.8%
300–499	9.6%	15.8%
500–999	9.0%	10.5%
1000–1999	4.6%	15.8%
2000–2999	0.9%	5.3%
3000–4999	0.8%	5.3%
More than 5000	0.6%	5.3%

Thus, my sample (admittedly rather small) still is fairly representative of the largest 3000 firms in Hungary, although it is overrepresentative of the larger firms.

One can also compare this to the distribution of sizes of firms in the entire economy as provided by the Hungarian central statistics office:

	Number of employees	*All firms*	*My cases*
Type Size A	11	<96.9%	0.0%
Type Size B	11–20	1.56%	5.3%
Type Size C	21–50	0.87%	15.8%
Type Size D	51–300	0.55%	26.3%
Type Size E	>300	0.11%	47.4%

Clearly, my firm case studies represent a good cross-section of the Hungarian economy in terms of size, representing a much greater proportion of larger firms. Their activity is also spread over many of the major sectors of the Hungarian economy.

THE CZECH REPUBLIC

	Activity	Number of Employees
Case 1	Agricultural software & misc.	600
Case 2	Computer assembly & sales	31
Case 3	Large engine manufacturer	500
Case 4	Press agency	230
Case 5	Holding company chem, pharm, petro	about 10,000
Case 6	Chemical trading	560
Case 7	Chemical importer	39
Case 8	Holding company agricultral imports	340
Case 9	Retailing company	400
Case 10	Branch of multi-national computer company	160
Case 11	Bank (one of the "big four")	4325
Case 12	Investment fund & broker	Over 5000 in over 70 companies that are at least partially owned
Case 13	Private TV station	400
Case 14	Travel agency	22,000
Case 15	Travel information service	10
Case 16	Pharmaceutical company	1300
Case 17	Chemical importer and distributer	40

Figures for holding companies include employees of all companies in the holding company. I believe the firms in my sample represent the "commanding heights" of the postcommunist Czech economy.

In the following, I compare the size breakdown of the largest 3110 manufacturing enterprises in the Czech Republic in 1994 to the breakdown of my sample of case studies.

Number of Employees	Total Population Czech Manufacturing 1994	My Sample (N=17)
Less than 25	0%	3.7%
25–99	39%	11.1%
100–299	32%	7.4%
300–499	11%	7.4%
500–999	9%	11.1%
1000–1999	5%	3.7%
2000–2999	2%	0%
3000–4999	1%	3.7%
More than 5000	1%	11.1%

SLOVAKIA

Company type	Number of employees
Case 1 Chemical company	3000
Case 2 Diesel engine	400
Case 3 Chocolate maker	800
Case 4 Travel agency	200
Case 5 Agribusiness	100
Case 6 Water and sewage public utility	2900
Case 7 Electronics audio and visual equipment, public address and broadcasting systems	200
Case 8 Automobile engines, gear boxes, axles	1200
Case 9 Telecommunication company	37,000
Case 10 Private bank	100

Appendix 4

Branch of Economy by at Least 30% Foreign Ownership

	Less than 30% *Foreign ownership*	*At least 30%* *Foreign ownership*	*Total*
Industry	74.0%	26.0%	404
Building	84.0%	16.0%	75
Agriculture	94.5%	5.5%	110
Transport	87.5%	12.5%	40
Commerce	75.6%	24.4%	238
Personal services	86.7%	13.3%	15
Financial	69.2%	30.8%	13
Other services	78.3%	21.7%	69
Health	66.7%	33.3%	3
Education	84.6%	15.4%	26
Politics	0%	100%	1
Other	66.7%	33.3%	6
Total	78.5%	21.5%	1000

Appendix 5

Previous Ownership by at Least 30% Current Foreign Ownership

Previous ownership	Less than 30% current foreign ownership	At least 30% current foreign ownership	Total
Full state	86.9%	13.1%	465
Partial state	70.6%	29.4%	68
No state	87.1%	12.9%	155
Average	85.3%	14.7%	688

Appendix 6

Previous Organizational Form by at Least 30% Foreign Ownership

	Less than 30% foreign ownership	At least 30% foreign ownership	Total
State	87.5%	12.5%	361
Coop	94.7%	5.3%	76
State budget	100%	0%	20
Limited company	59.4%	40.6%	64
Stock company	84.2%	15.8%	38
Small coop	94.7%	5.1%	39
Partnership	81.8%	18.2%	22
Foundation	100.0%	0%	1
Private	75.0%	25.0%	4
Other	95.0%	5.0%	20
Total number	587%	101%	688
Average	85.3%	14.7%	

Appendix 7

Previous Organizational Form by MEBO

	Less than 30% MEBO	At least 30% MEBO	Total
State	88.4	11.6	361
Coop	34.2	65.8	76
State budget	95.0	5.0	20
Limited company	73.4	26.6	64
Stock company	84.2	15.8	38
Small coop	30.4	68.2	39
Joint-venture	86.0	14.0	43
Partnership	54.5	45.5	22
Foundation	0	100.0	1
Private	50.0	50.0	4
Other	95.0	5.0	20
Total number	587	101	688
Average	85.3	14.7	100

Appendix 8

Sectoral Distribution of MEBOs

	Less than 30% MEBO	At least 30% MEBO	Total
Industry	80.9%	19.1%	404
Building	64.0%	36.0%	75
Agriculture	62.7%	37.3%	110
Transportation	82.5%	17.5%	40
Commerce	77.7%	22.3%	238
Personal service	80.0%	20.0%	15
Financial service	69.2%	30.8%	13
Other service	85.5%	14.5%	69
Health	88.1%	11.9%	3
Education	88.5%	11.5%	26
Politics	100.0%	0.0%	1
Other	83.5%	16.5%	6
Average	77.4%	22.6%	1000

Appendix 9

Reported Clientelism among MEBOs

Help from Friend or Relation to Get Credit by MEBO

	Less than 30% MEBO	*At least 30% MEBO*	*Total*
No help	80.0%	20.0%	641
Help	72.7%	27.3%	359
Average	77.4%	22.6%	1000

Help from Friend or Relation for Purchases by MEBO

	Less than 30% MEBO	*At least 30% MEBO*	*Total*
No help	82.4%	17.6%	370
Help	74.5%	25.5%	631
Average	77.4%	22.6%	1001

Help from Friend or Relation for Sales by MEBO

	Less than 30% MEBO	*At least 30% MEBO*	*Total*
No help	82.3%	17.7%	434
Help	73.7%	26.3%	567
Average	77.4%	22.6%	1001

Help from Friend or Relation for Custom Tax by MEBO

	Less than 30% MEBO	*At least 30% MEBO*	*Total*
No Help	79.9%	20.3%	627
Help	73.5%	26.5%	374
Average	77.4%	22.6%	1001

Personal Connection to the Ministry of Finance by MEBO

	Less than 30% MEBO	*At least 30% MEBO*	*Total*
No connection	75.1%	24.9%	810
Connection	87.4%	12.6%	199
Average	77.4%	22.6%	1000

Appendix 10

Domestic Dependence by MEBO

	Less than 30% MEBO	At least 30% MEBO	Total
Low	83.5%	16.5%	127
Medium	79.1%	20.9%	172
High	79.5%	20.5%	219
Very High	73.9%	26.1%	518
Average	77.4%	22.6%	1001

Appendix 11

State Dependence by MEBO

	Less than 30% MEBO	At least 30% Total MEBO	
Low	75.3%	24.7%	522
Medium	78.2%	21.8%	165
High	79.4%	20.6%	160
Very High	81.3%	18.7%	154
Average	77.4%	22.6%	1001

Bibliography

Alchian, Armen, and Harold Demsetz. 1972. "Production, Information Costs, and Economic Organization." *American Economic Review* 57: 777–95.

Andorka, Rudolf. 1993. "The Socialist System and its Collapse in Hungary: An Interpretation in Terms of Modernization Theory." *International Sociology* 8(3): 317–37. September.

Apter, David. 1990. *Rethinking Development: Modernization, Dependency, and Post Modern Politics.* New York: Sage.

Bakos, Gabor. 1995. "Hungary's Road to Privatization." In *Privatization and Foreign Investment in Eastern Europe*, ed. Iliana Zloch-Christy. Westport CT: Praeger Publishers.

Baran, Paul. 1957. *The Political Economy of Growth.* New York: Monthly Review Press.

Bartha, Atilla. 1996. "Bank Leaders as the Inner Circle of Hungarian Economic Elite." Paper presented at the *Euroconference on Doing Social Research: Problems and Challenges.* Nurnberg, March 6–9.

Belka, Marek, et al. 1993. "Country Overview Study: Poland." *European Economics* 31(5): 19–62.

Berle, Adolf, and Gardiner Means. 1968 [1932]. *The Modern Corporation and Private Property.* New York: Harcourt.

Bettelheim, Charles. 1976 [1970]. *Economic Calculations and Forms of Property.* Trans. John Taylor. London: Routledge and Kegal Paul.

Blanchard, Olivier, Maxim Boycko, Marek Dabrowski, Rudiger Dornbusch, Richard Layard, and Andrei Shleifer. 1993. *Post-Communist Reform: Pain and Progress.* Cambridge, MA: MIT Press.

Bogetic, Zeljko. 1993. "The Role of Employee Ownership in Privatization and State Enterprises in Eastern and Central Europe." *Europe-Asia Studies* 45(3): 463–81.

Bornschier, Volker, and Christopher Chase-Dunn. 1985. *Multinational Corporations and Underdevelopment.* Westport, CT: Praeger Publishers.

Bourdieu, P. 1977. "Cultural Reproduction and Social Reproduction." In *Power and Ideology in Education*, ed. J. Karabel and A. H. Halsey. Oxford University Press. 487–511.

Bradshaw, York. 1987. "Urbanization and Underdevelopment: A Global Study of Modernization, Urban Bias, and Economic Dependency." *American Sociological Review* 52: 224–39.

Brenner, Robert. 1976. "Agrarian Class Structure and Economic Development in Pre-Industrial England," *Past and Present*, no. 70, 30–75.

———. 1983. *Marx's First Model of the Transition to Capitalism.* Mimeo.

———. 1986. "The Social Basis of Economic Growth." In *Analytical Marxism*, ed. E. O. Write and Jon Elster. Madison: University of Wisconsin Press.

Burawoy, Michael. 1986. *The Radiant Past: Ideology and Reality in Hungary's Road to Capitalism.* Chicago: Univerisity of Chicago Press.

———. 1997. "What is Russia and Where is it Going? Towards a Theory of Economic Involution." Paper presented at the *Comparative Social Analysis Workshop.* UCLA, January.

Burawoy, Michael, and Janos Lukacs. 1985. "Mythologies of Work: A Comparison of Firms in State Socialism and Advanced Capitalism." *American Sociological Review* 12(50): 723–37.

Burawoy, Michael, and Peter Krotov. 1992. "The Soviet Transition From Socialism to Capitalism: Worker Control and Economic Bargaining." *American Sociological Review* 57: 16–38.

Campeanu, Pavel [Casals]. 1980. *Syncretic Society.* Armonk, NY: M. E. Sharpe.

Capek, Ales, and Pavel Mertlik. 1996. "Organizational Change and Financial Restructuring in Czech Manufacturing Enterprises 1990–1995." Czech National Bank Institute of Economics. Mimeo.

Cardoso, Fernando, and Enzo Faletto. 1979. *Dependency and Development in Latin America.* University of California Press.

Carlin, Wendy, Jon Van Reenen, and Toby Wolfe. 1994. *Enterprise Restructuring in the Transition: An Analytical Survey of the Case Study Evidence from Central and Eastern Europe.* Working Paper No. 14. London: European Bank for Reconstruction and Development.

———. 1995. "Enterprise Restructuring in Early Transition: The Case Study Evidence from Central and Eastern Europe." *Economics of Transition* 3: 427–58.

Chandler, Alfred. 1970. *Strategy and Structure.* Cambridge, MA: Harvard University Press.

Caves, Richard. 1964. *American Industry: Structure, Conduct, Performance.* Englewood Cliffs, NJ: Prentice-Hall.

Chase-Dunn, Christopher. 1975. "The Effects of International Economic Dependence on Development and Inequality: A Cross-National Study." *American Sociological Review* 40: 720–38.

Chenery, Hollis, and Peter Eckstein. 1970. "Development Alternatives for Latin America." *Journal of Political Economy* 78: 966–1006.

Chirot, Daniel. 1995. "Modernization Happened, Didn't It?" Paper presented at the Center for Social Theory and Comparative History, UCLA.

Coase, Ronald. 1937. "The Nature of the Firm." Economica 4: 386-405

Csaki, Gyorgy. 1995. "Foreign Direst Investment in Hungary." In *Privatization and Foreign Investment in Eastern Europe*, ed. Iliana Zloch-Christy. Westport, CT: Praeger.

Dabrowski, J., M. Federowicz, and A. Levitas. 1991. "Polish State Enterprises and the Property of Performance: Stabilization, Marketization, Privatization." *Politics and Society* 19: 403–38.

Dobosiewicz, Zbigniew. 1992. *Foreign Investment in Eastern Europe*. New York: Routledge.

Demsetz, Harold. 1967. "Towards a Theory of Property Rights." *American Economic Review* 57 (May): 347–59.

———. 1988. "The Theory of the Firm Revisited." *Journal of Law, Economics and Organization* 4: 141–62.

Demsetz, Harold, and Kenneth Lehn. 1985. "The Structure of Corporate Ownership; Causes and Consequences," *Journal of Political Economy* 93: 1155-77.

Dimagio, Paul J. and Walter W. Powell. 1983. "Institutional Isomorphism." *American Sociological Review*. v. 48 n. 2 p. 147-160.

Domhoff, G. William. 1986. *Who Rules America Now? A View from the 1980's*. New York: Simon and Schuster.

Dunning, John. 1993. "The Prospects for Foreign Direct Investment in Eastern Europe." In *Foreign Investment in Central and Eastern Europe*. eds. Patrick Artisen, Matija Rojec, and Marjan Svetlicic. New York: St. Martin's Press.

Earle, John, Roman Frydman, and Andrzej Rapaczynski, eds. 1993. *Privatization in the Transition to a Market Economy: Studies of Preconditions and Policies in Eastern Europe*. New York: St. Martin's Press.

Economist Intelligence Unit. "Hungary: Country Report." Fourth quarter 1996 and first quarter 1998.

Ellerman, David, ed. 1993. *Management and Employee Buy-Outs as a Technique of Privatization*. Ljubljana: Central and Eastern European Privatization Network.

Evans, Peter, and Michael Timberlake. 1980. "Dependence, Inequality, and the Growth of the Tertiary: A Comparative Analysis of Less Developed Countries." *American Sociological Review* 45: 531–51.

Eyal, Gil. 1997. "The Ideology of Post-Communist Elites." Manuscript.

Eyal, Gil, Ivan Szelenyi, and Eleanor Townsley. 1998. *Making Capitalism without Capitalists: Class Formation and Elite Struggles in Post-Communist Central Europe*. London: Verso.

———. Forthcoming. *Capitalism Without Capitalists*. London: Verso.

Fama, Eugene, and Michael Jensen. 1983a. "Agency Problems and Residual Claims." *Journal of Law and Economics* 26: 327–42.

———. 1983b. "Separation of Ownership and Control." *Journal of Law and Economics* 26: 300–25.

Faur, Tivadar. 1993. "Foreign Capital in Hungary's privatization." In *Privatization in the Transition to a Market Economy: Studies of Preconditions and Policies in Eastern Europe*, ed. John Earl, Roman Frydman and Andrzej Rapaczynski. New York: St. Martin's Press.

Fischer, Stanley, and Alan Gelb. 1991. "The Process of Socialist Economic Transformation." *Journal of Economic Perspectives* 4: 91–106.

Fligstein, Neil. 1990. *The Transformation of Corporate Control*. Cambridge, MA: Harvard University Press.

Fodor, Eva, and Eric Hanley. 1996. *Voting in Postcommunist Society*. Manuscript.

Frank, Andre Gunther. 1967. *Capitalism and Underdevelopment in Latin America*. New York: Monthly Review Press.

———. 1969. Latin America: *Underdevelopment of Revolution*. New York: Monthly Review Press

———. 1970. *Capitalism and Underdevelopment of Revolution*. New York: Monthly Review Press.

———. 1972. "Sociology of Development and the Underdevelopment of Sociology." In *Dependence and Underdevelopment: Latin American Political Economy*, eds. James Cockroft, Frank Johnson, and Dale Johnson, 321-397. (Garden City, NJ:Doubleday and Co. Inc.)

Frydman, Roman, Kenneth Murphy, and Andrej Rapaczynski. 1996. "Capitalism with a Camraderly Face," *Magyar Hirlap* (March 8): 9.

Fukuyama, Francis. 1992. *The End Of History and the Last Man*. Toronto: Maxwell Macmillan.

Furubotn, E., and S. Perjovich, eds. 1974. *The Economics of Property Rights*. Cambridge, MA: Ballinger.

Galtung, Johan. 1971. "A Structural Theory of Imperialism." *Journal of Peace Research* 8: 81–117.

Giddens, Anthony. 1984. *The Constitution of Society*. Cambridge: Polity Press.

Gowan, Peter. 1995. "Neo-Liberal Theory and Practice for Eastern Europe." *New Left Review* 213: 3–60.

Granoveter, Mark. 1985. "Economic Action and Social Structure: The Problem of Embeddedness." *American Journal of Sociology* 91: 481–510.

Hamar, J. 1994. "Foreign Direct Investment and Privatization in Hungary." *Acta Oeconomica* 46(1–2): 189–212.

Hankiss, Elemer. 1990. *East European Alternatives*. Oxford: Clarendon Press.

Hanley, Eric. 1996. "Self-Employment in Post-Communist Europe: A Refuge from Poverty or the Emergence of a New Petty Bourgeoisie?" Mimeo. Institute of Sociology, Czech Academy of Sciences.

Hannan, Michael. 1989. *Organizational Ecology*. Cambridge, MA: Harvard University Press.

Hannan, Michael T. and John Freeman. 1977. "The Population Ecology of Organizations." *American Journal of Sociology* 82: 924–64.

Havas, Gabor, J. Ladanyi, and Ivan Szelenyi. 1996. *The Making of the East European Underclass: The Case of a Gypsy Village Ghetto*. Mimeo.

Hoselitz, B.F. 1965. *Sociological Aspects of Economic Growth*. New York: Free Press.

Hovanyi, Gabor. 1993–94. Edited and revised by Adam Torok. "Industry Case Study: Hungary Electronics Industry. Radio Radio and Electrical Works: 'The Whiz Kid Grows Old?'" *European Economics* 31(6) 101–13

Jensen, Michael C., and William H. Meckling. 1976. "Theory of the Firm: Managerial Behavior, Agency Costs and Ownership Structure." *Journal of Financial Economics* 4(4): 305–60.

Karsai, Judith, and Mike Write. 1994. "Accountability, Governance and Finance in Hungarian Buy-Outs." *Europe-Asia Studies* 46(6): 997–1016.

Kenway, Peter and Eva Klacova. 1996. "The Web of Cross-Ownership among Czech Financial Intermediaries: An Assessment." *Europe-Asia Studies* 48(5): 797–809.

Knight, Robin. 1994. "Sewing up Central Europe's Work Force." *U.S. News & World Report* (Aug. 29/Sept. 5): 47–49.

Konrad, George and Ivan Szelenyi. 1979. *Intellectuals on the Road to Class Power.* New York: Harcourt Brace and Jovanovich.

———. 1991. "Intellectuals and Domination under Post-Communism." In *Social Theory for a Changing Society*, ed. James Coleman and Pierre Bourdieu. Boulder: Westview Press. 337–61.

Kornai, Janos. 1980. *Economics of Shortage.* Amsterdam, New York, Oxford: North Holland Publishing Company.

Kosolowski, Rey. 1992. "Market Institutions, East European Reform, and Economic Theory." *Journal of Economic Issues* 26: 673–705.

Kuffner, K. 1988. "English the Common Language of Europeans." *International Management* 4(42): 24–29.

Landsburg, Martin. 1979. "Export-Led Industrialization in the Third World: Manufacturing Imperialism." *Review of Radical Political Economics* 11: 50–63.

Lipton, David and Jeffrey D. Sachs. 1990. "Creating a Market Economy in Eastern Europe: The Case of Poland." *Brookings Paper on Economic Activity* 1.

London, Bruce. 1987. "Structural Determinants of Third World Urban Change: An Ecological and Political Economic Analysis." *American Sociological Review* 52: 28–43.

———. 1988. "Dependence, Distorted Development, and Fertility Trends in Noncore Nations: A Structural Analysis of Cross-National Data." *American Sociological Review* 53: 606–18.

Mann, Catherine L. 1991. "Industry Restructuring in East-Central Europe: The Challenge and the Role for Foreign Investment." *American Economic Review* 81 (May): 181–84.

Mann, Michael. 1986. *The Sources of Social Power.* New York: Cambridge University Press.

March, James G., and Herbert A. Simon. 1958. *Organizations.* New York: Wiley.

Matesova, Jana. 1993–94. "Country Overview Study: Czech and Slovak Republics. 'Will the Manufacturing Heart Beat Again?'" *European Economics* 31(6): 3–35.

———. 1994. "Industry Case Study: Czech and Slovak Republics Textile/Cloth: Veba Broumov—'The King of a Declining Industry'" *European Economics* 31(6): 36–51.

Matza, David. 1979. *Becoming Deviant.* Englewood Cliffs, NJ: Prentice Hall.

Matzner, Egon. 1995. Market Making and Market Destruction. Paper prepared for the 3rd AGENDA Workshop on *Lessons from Transformation.* Vienna.

McClelland, David. 1964. "Business Drive and National Achievement." In *Social Change*, ed. Amitai Etzioni and Eva Etzioni, 165–78. New York: Basic Books.

Mejstrik, Michal. 1995. "Economic Transformation, Privatization, and Foreign Investment in the Czech Republic." In *Privatization and Foreign Investment in Eastern Europe*, ed. Iliana Zloch-Christy. Westport, CT: Praeger Publishers.

Mertlik, Pavel. 1995. *The Czech Canning Industry.* Gelsenkirchen/Prague: Institut Arbeit und Technik.

———. 1996 "The Czech Republic." In *The Future of Industry in Central and Eastern Europe*, ed. Brigitta Widmaier, and Wolfgang Potratz. Gelsenkirchen: Institut Arbeit und Technik.

Mihalyi, Peter. 1992. "Privatization in Hungary." Institute of Economics Hungarian Academy of Sciences. Discussion Papers #3, Budapest.

Mills, C. Wright. 1956. *The Power Elite*. New York: Oxford University Press.

Nee, Victor. 1989. "A Theory of Market Transition: From Redistribution to Markets in State Socialism." *American Sociological Review* 54: 663–81.

———. 1991. "Social Inequalities in Reforming State Socialism." *American Sociological Review* 56: 267–82.

———. 1992a. "Sleeping with the Enemy: Why Communists Love the Market." *Cornell Working Papers on the Transition from State Socialism*, 92.1. Ithaca, NY: Mario Einudi Center for International Studies.

———. 1992b. "Organizational Dynamics of Market Transition: Hybrid Forms, Property Rights, and Mixed Economy in China." *Administrative Science Quarterly* 37: 1–27.

———. 1992. "Organizational Dynamics of Market Transition." *Administrative Science Quarterly* 37: 1-27.

———. 1996. "The Emergence of a Market Society: Changing Mechanisms of Stratification in China." *American Journal of Sociology* 101: 908-49.

North, Douglas. 1990. *Structure and Change in Economic History*. New York: Norton and Company.

Nuti, M. 1990. "Privatization of Socialist Economies: General Issues and the Polish Case." Paper presented at the *1st Conference of the European Association for Comparative Economic Studies*, Verona, 27–29 September.

OECD Economic Outlook. 1995.

Oi, Jean C. 1992. "Fiscal Reform and the Economic Foundations of Local State Corporatism in China." *World Politics* 45.1 (October): 99–126.

Perrow, Charles. 1986. *Complex Organizations*: A Critical Essay. 3d. ed. New York: Random House.

Polanyi, Karl. 1957 [1944]. *The Great Transformation*. Boston: Beacon Press.

Powell, Walter, and Laurel Smith-Doer. 1994. "Networks and Economic Life." In *Handbook of Economic Sociology*, eds. Richard Swedberg and Neil J. Smelser, 368-402. (Princeton, NJ: Princeton University Press)

Pratt, John, and Richard Zeckhauser. 1986. *Principals and Agents*. Boston: HBS Press.

Rona-Tas, Ákos. 1994. "The First Shall be Last? Entrepreneurship and the Communist Cadres in the Transition form Socialism." *American Journal of Sociology* 100: 40–69.

———. 1996. "The Czech New Wave: The Third Wave of Privatization and the Role of the State in the Czech Republic." Paper presented at the Workshop on Comparative Sociology, UCLA.

Roy, William G. 1997. *Socializing Capital*. Princeton, NJ: Princeton University Press.

Sachs, J., and D. Lipton. 1990. "Poland's Economic Reform." *Foreign Affairs* (Summer): 47–66.

Sachs, Jeffrey. 1991. "The Economic Tranformation of Eastern Europe: The Case of Poland." (The Frank E. Seidman Distinguished Award in Political Economy. Acceptance paper by Jeffrey Sachs.) Memphis, TN: P. K. Seidman Foundation.

Sahlins, Marshall. 1991. "The Return of the Event, Again; With Reflections on the Beginnings of the Great Fijian War of 1843 and 1855 between the Kingdoms of Bau and Rewa." In *Clio in Oceana: Toward a Historical Anthropology*, ed. Aletta Biersack. Washington: Smithsonian Institute Press.

Scherer, F. M., and David Ross. 1990. *Industrial Market Structure and Economic Performance.* 3d. ed. Boston: Houghton Mifflin.

Schlucter, W. 1989. *Rationalism, Religion, and Domination.* Berkeley and Los Angeles: The University of California Press.

Schumpeter, Joseph. 1975 [1942]. *Capitalism, Socialism and Democracy.* New York: Harper.

Sewell, William H. Jr., 1992a. "Three Temporalities: Toward an Eventful Sociology. In *The Historic Turn in the Human Sciences*, ed. Terrence J. McDonald. Ann Arbor: University of Michigan Press.

———. 1992b. "A Theory of Structure: Duality, Agency, and Transformation." *American Journal of Sociology* 98: 1–29.

Staniszkis, Jadwiga. 1991. *The Dynamics of Breakthrough.* Berkeley: University of California Press.

Stark, David. 1989. "Coexisting Organizational Forms in Hungary's Emerging Mixed Economy." In *Remaking the Economic Institutions of Socialism: China and Europe*, 137–168, ed. Victor Nee and David Stark. Stanford: Stanford University Press.

———. 1992. Path Dependency and Privatization Strategies in East-Central Europe." *East European Politics and Societies* 6(1).

———. 1993. "Recombinant Property in European Capitalism." Mimeo.

———. 1996. "Recombinant Property in European Capitalism," *American Journal of Sociology* 101(5): 993–1027.

Stark, David, and Laszlo Bruszt. 1995. "Inter-Enterprise Ownership Networks in the Postsocialist Transformation." Paper presented on "Dynamics of Industrial Transformation: East Central European and East Asian Comparisons."

Svetlicic, Marjan, Patrick Artisien, and Matija Rojec. 1993. "Foreign Direct Investment in Central and Eastern Europe: An Overview." In *Foreign Investment in Central and Eastern Europe*, eds. Patrick Artisen, Matija Rojec and Marjan Svetlicic. New York: St. Martin's Press.

Szalai, Erzsébet. 1992. *Gazdaság és hatalom* (Economy and Power). Budapest: Aula.

———. 1994. "The Power Structure in Hungary after the Political Transition." In *The New Great Transformation?*, ed. Christopher G. A. Bryant and Edmund Mokrzycki. Routledge: New York.

Szelenyi, Ivan. 1981. "The Relative Autonomy of the State or State Mode of Production?" In *Urbanization and Urban Planning*, ed. M. J. Dear and A. J. Scott, 565–91. London: Methuen.

———. 1982. "The Intelligentsia in the Class Structure of State-Socialist Societies." *American Journal of Sociology* 88: 287–326.

———. 1986–87. "The Prospects and Limits of the East European New Class Project: an Auto-Critical Reflection on The Intellectuals on the Road to Class Power." *Politics and Society* 15(2): 103–44.

———. 1995. "The Rise of Managerialism: 'The New Class' After the Fall of Communism." Discussion Paper 16. Collegium Budapest: Public Lecture Series.

Szelenyi, Ivan, and Eric Costello. 1996. "The Market Transition Debate: Towards a Synthesis." *American Journal of Sociology* 101: 1082-96.

Szelenyi, Ivan, and Bill Martin. 1988. "Three Waves of New Class Theory." *Theory and Society* 17: 645–67.

Szelenyi, Ivan, and Balasz Szelenyi. 1995. "Why Socialism Failed." *Theory and Society* 23: 211–31.

Szelenyi, Ivan, and Szonja Szelenyi. 1990. "Az elite cirkulácilója?" (Circulation of Elites?) *Kritika.*

Timberlake, Michael, and Jeffrey Kentor. 1983. "Economic Dependence, Overurbanization, and Economic Growth: A Study of Less Developed Countries." *Sociological Quarterly* 24: 489–507.

UNCTAD (United Nations Conference on Trade and Development). World Investment Report 1995. New York.

United Nations. 1996. *World Investment Report: Investment, Trade and International Policy Arrangements.* New York and Geneva.

Voska, Eva. 1993. "Spontaneous Privatization in Hungary," In *Privatization in the Transition to a Market Economy: Studies of Preconditions and Policies in Eastern Europe*, ed. John S. Earl, Roman Frydman and Andrzej Rapaczynski. New York: St. Martin's Press.

———. 1994 "The Revival of Redistribution in Hungary," *Acta Oeconomica* 46(1–2): 63–78.

Walder, Andrew. 1992a. "Property Rights and Stratification in Socialist Redistributive Economics." *American Sociological Review* 57: 524–39.

———. 1992b. "Markets and Political Change in Rural China: A Property Rights Analysis."

———. 1992c. "Corporate Organization and Local State Property Rights: The Chinese Alternative to Privatization."

Wallerstein, Immanuel. 1974. *The Modern World-System: Capitalist Agriculture and the Origins of European World-Economy in the Sixteenth Century.* New York: Academic Press.

Walters, Alan. 1990. "How Fast Can Market Economies Be Introduced?" European Business Forum, Financial Times Conference, November 26–27.

Weber, Max. 1946. *From Max Weber*, eds. H.H. Gerth and C.Wright Mills. New York: Oxford University Press.

Weber, Max. 1978 [1922]. *Economy and Society.* Berkeley: University of California Press.

Widmaier, Brigitta, and Wolfgang Potratz. 1996. *The Future of Industry in Central and Eastern Europe.* Gelsenkirchen: Institut Arbeit und Technik.

Williamson, Oliver. 1975. *Markets and Hierarchies: Analysis and Antitrust Implications.* New York: Free Press.

———. 1981. "The Economics of Organization: The Transaction Cost Approach." *American Journal of Sociology* 87: 548–77.

Williamson, Oliver E. 1985. *The Economic Institutions of Capitalism.* New York: Free Press.

Young, David G. 1993. "Foreign Direct Investment in Hungary." In *Foreign Investment in Central and Eastern Europe*, ed. Patrick Artisen, Matija Rojec, and Marjan Svetlicic, 109–122. New York: St. Martin's Press.

Zeitlin, Maurice, 1974. "Corporate Ownership and Control: The Large Corporation and the Capitalist Class." *American Journal of Sociology* 89: 1073–1119.

Zeitlin, Maurice and Richard E. Ratcliff. 1984. *The Civil Wars of Chile: The Bourgeois Revolutions That Never Were*. Princeton: Princeton University Press.

———. 1988. *Landlords and Capitalists: The Dominant Class of Chile*. Princeton: Princeton University Press.

Zemplinerova, Alena, Radek Lastovicka, and Anton Marcincin. 1995. "Restructuring of Czech Manufacturing Enterprises: An Empirical Study." *Working Paper Series*. CERGE-EI: Prague.

Zloch-Christy, Iliana, ed. 1995. *Privatization and Foreign Investment in Eastern Europe*. Westport, CT: Praeger Publishers.

Index

About the Author

Lawrence Peter King is Assistant Professor of Sociology at Yale University. His research and teaching focus on the areas of comparative historical sociology, political and economic sociology, development, complex organizations, and sociological theory. Among his publications is *The Rise and Fall of the New Class* (with Ivan Szelenyi).